Praise for *Guarded by Christ*

In days of terror and horror, when danger prevails and safety fails, we all need a place of security, a sure protector who will not yield. That person is our God, and Heather Holleman leads us to know Him in a fresh, even transforming way: as the God who guards us. She unveils the reality of who He is and how we are safe with Him, just when we need such a certainty.

JUDY DOUGLASS
Director, Women's Resources, Campus Crusade for Christ
International (Cru); author of *Letters to My Children: Secrets of Success*

Why do I *love* Heather Holleman's new book? Yes, it is authentically honest and refreshingly perceptive, but that is not why I love it. Heather wrote *Guarded by Christ* because *guard* became her new favorite word in Scripture. As she shared from her heart, *guard* became my new favorite biblical word too! Do you desire to know how God guards your soul? Read this book and you will find yourself praying, "Thank You, God, for all the ways You guard me!"

LINDA DILLOW
Author of *Calm My Anxious Heart* and *Satisfy My Thirsty Soul*;
coauthor of *Surprised by the Healer*

guarded *by Christ*

KNOWING THE GOD WHO
RESCUES AND KEEPS US

heather holleman

MOODY PUBLISHERS

CHICAGO

© 2016 by
HEATHER HOLLEMAN

All Scripture quotations, unless otherwise indicated, are taken from the Holy Bible, New International Version®, NIV®. Copyright © 1973, 1978, 1984, 2011 by Biblica, Inc.™ Used by permission of Zondervan. All rights reserved worldwide. www.zondervan.com. The "NIV" and "New International Version" are trademarks registered in the United States Patent and Trademark Office by Biblica, Inc.™

Scripture quotations marked ESV are from The Holy Bible, English Standard Version® (ESV®), copyright © 2001 by Crossway, a publishing ministry of Good News Publishers. Used by permission. All rights reserved.

Scripture quotations marked NASB are taken from the New American Standard Bible®, Copyright © 1960, 1962, 1963, 1968, 1971, 1972, 1973, 1975, 1977, 1995 by The Lockman Foundation. Used by permission. (www.Lockman.org)

Scripture quotations marked NLT are taken from the Holy Bible, New Living Translation, copyright © 1996, 2004, 2007, 2013 by Tyndale House Foundation. Used by permission of Tyndale House Publishers, Inc., Carol Stream, Illinois 60188. All rights reserved.

Emphasis in Scripture has been added by the author.

Published in association with the literary agency of D.C. Jacobson and Associates LLC, 537 SE Ash Street, Suite 203, Portland, OR 97214.

Edited by Pam Pugh
Interior design: Ragont Design
Author photo: BowerShots Photography
Cover design: Erik M. Peterson
Cover image of building copyright © 2011 by Alistair Gibbs / iStock (18569124). All rights reserved.

Library of Congress Cataloging-in-Publication Data

Names: Holleman, Heather, author.
Title: Guarded by Christ : knowing the God who rescues and keeps us / Heather Holleman.
Description: Chicago, IL : Moody Publishers, 2016. | Includes bibliographical references.
Identifiers: LCCN 2016021663 (print) | LCCN 2016023888 (ebook) | ISBN 9780802414878 | ISBN 9780802494818 ()
Subjects: LCSH: Christian women--Religious life. | Christian life.
Classification: LCC BV4527 .H643 2016 (print) | LCC BV4527 (ebook) | DDC 248.8/43--dc23
LC record available at https://lccn.loc.gov/2016021663

ISBN: 978-0-8024-1487-8

We hope you enjoy this book from Moody Publishers. Our goal is to provide high-quality, thought-provoking books and products that connect truth to your real needs and challenges. For more information on other books and products written and produced from a biblical perspective, go to www.moodypublishers.com or write to:

Moody Publishers
820 N. LaSalle Boulevard
Chicago, IL 60610

1 3 5 7 9 10 8 6 4 2

For my big sister, Melissa Kish

CONTENTS

ABOUT THE COVER

Tintern Abbey, built in 1131, rests on the River Wye near Chepstow, Wales. As a site of national importance and pilgrimage, the abbey once thrived as a prosperous destination for those seeking the religious life. The poet William Wordsworth wrote about this abbey in "Lines Composed a Few Miles above Tintern Abbey, July 13, 1798" because the memory of the abbey brought "tranquil restoration" to his soul and a sublime sense of something much larger than himself. Like the towers and fortresses King David called to mind to remember God's guarding care, Tintern Abbey stands today as a marvelous image of worship, peace, and refuge.

PART ONE

—⁓—

OUR GUARDING GOD

CHAPTER I

TRUE PLACES

It is not down in any map; true places never are.
—HERMAN MELVILLE IN *MOBY DICK*

The summer before I turned forty years old, I learned something about my storm-tossed soul that ushered in a fresh experience of Jesus.

I sat on a sagging bed in a rented apartment where my family had traveled for a ministry assignment in a city over a thousand miles from home. The dirty bedroom with cracked walls and carpet stains offered the early morning setting where I was about to read a passage of Scripture that wouldn't let me go. I tied my hair back in a rubber band—the kind that come in packs of twenty but can rarely be found when needed—and adjusted my glasses. I heard our children, now in the preteen and teenage years, scrambling to get dressed. I stretched out a hand to find a mug and gulped down the coffee with hazelnut creamer my husband had delivered like it was vital medication for the ailment called *waking up in the morning.* I flipped open the Bible, ready to pour all this exhaustion, anxiety, and homesickness onto any words that could neutralize these emotions.

I turned to Psalm 97 and read from verse 10 that God "guards the lives of his faithful ones."

I stared at that word—*guards*—as if seeing it for the first time.

I swallowed more coffee. I kept staring.

It seemed like such a clear, easy statement to understand—*God guards the lives of His faithful ones*—and yet I wasn't sure I fully got it. Believers in Jesus were counted as His faithful ones, and this included me, but what could it mean that God guards us? This verb presented a secure and safe reality, but in my Christian life, I rarely felt *secure*. If God was guarding me, I certainly didn't know how to experience this in any tangible form. The questions persisted like termites chewing at my soul: Is God guarding us? Where is He guarding us? For what purpose?

The simple verb ignited a firestorm of urgent questions within because I knew I wasn't living as one guarded by God. Someone God guards surely wouldn't feel this unstable, unsettled, and immature.

I refilled the mug and began the search that would profoundly change my soul, transforming my inner being into something stable, settled, and mature.

"Guards," is *shamar* in Hebrew, which means to hedge about, keep safe, protect, watch carefully, preserve. Usually *shamar* refers to the "keeping" of the law—guarding, observing, and carefully preserving God's words—but when used in multiple psalms, the word suggests a person fenced in an enclosure being carefully watched over and protected. The psalmists often connected God's guarding presence to a physical, surrounding location like this. King David, for example, asks God to guard him as he takes *refuge* in Him and makes Him his *fortress* (Psalms 16:1; 31:2).

Finally, the "lives" that God guards is actually the word for "souls," so a more precise translation of this phrase in Psalm 97 is "God guards the souls of His people."

But where is guarding happening? Where is this refuge?

Where is this fortress? Since it's not anything we can see with our eyes, how are we to think of it?

Searching the Scriptures to examine *what* God guards and *how* He guards it in us, I learned that the Bible presents us with a Savior who dwells in our inner being by the Holy Spirit and who imparts all the characteristics of God's guarding presence to our soul. I wanted to learn every aspect of what this guarding presence was like because I hadn't come to know Jesus like this. I knew Him as my salvation and that I was seated with him in the heavenly realms (Ephesians 2:6), but I didn't know Him as a *Guarding* God. I didn't know everything He was doing in my soul.

Could understanding more about our Guarding God help us as Christians "grow up in [our] salvation" (1 Peter 2:2) so we would become "thoroughly equipped" for the good works God had prepared for us to do (2 Timothy 3:17; Ephesians 2:10)? I wasn't sure what I would discover as I searched the Scriptures to learn more, but I just knew this: God was already beginning to transform me as I met Him as my Guarding God.

On the very day I prayed that God would teach me more about His guarding presence, I watched as my husband, Ashley, prepared our older daughter for her first day out alone in the city without us. While Ashley and I kept busy with ministry assignments in this new city, our younger daughter was enrolled in the camp provided. But our older had the freedom to choose some independent activities. For the first time in her life, she would ride her bike *alone* to meet her friends, enjoy a lunch out at a restaurant, and then spend the afternoon hanging out downtown. She was growing up—this was normal and right—but I wasn't ready.

Her dad delivered final instructions as he adjusted her helmet around her blond ponytail. I heard him remind her about her bike lock, wallet, and phone, but then all I could think about was losing her to kidnapping, traffic accident, or random disaster. I said good-bye and watched her pedal off from our apartment.

Then the anxiety came. I just knew something terrible would happen. I left for my seminary classes that were part of ministry training, trying desperately to focus on the lectures. During the day, the phone buzzed with several text messages. I plunged my hand into my bag, breathless and nervous each time. Was Sarah hurt? Was she missing? Had a flood come and swept her into a ravine?

The stream of messages came:

"She made it through the intersection! I see her!" Ashley texted. He even snapped a photograph; I could see that blond ponytail flying and those feet pedaling with confidence.

And later:

"She's with her friends! I'm going to 'accidentally' meet her and give her more money for lunch."

And later:

"She's in the restaurant. She's doing great! I see her."

All day long on that first day Sarah was without us, my husband trailed our daughter in the minivan, unseen by her. He was guarding her carefully, watching over all of her needs, and assuring her well-being. Sarah never knew her daddy was following her that first day on her own, but he was. He was there the whole time.

As I sat there with the phone, tears formed. I imagined the gentle whisper of God deep in my soul: "This is what it's like between you and Me. I guard you like this. I'm taking care of everything that concerns you."

And that simple verb, guard, became my new favorite word in Scripture.

As a writing instructor specializing in vivid verbs, I teach college freshmen that every verb they use should evoke a mood and an image. "Never waste a verb," I tell them, closing my eyes and tenting my hands together like we're sharing a sacred moment. When one of them uses a particularly vivid verb—perhaps assuage, embellish, or fritter—I clap with joy and might even hop up and down.

When we read the verb *guard*, we cannot help but feel protected, secure, important, kept close, and carefully observed. The verb feels demanding; it proclaims the urgent protection of a precious person. I stared again at the verb and then wrote down the truth: *God guards me. God guards me right now.*

A PERSON GOD GUARDS LIVES WITH *CONFIDENCE, PEACE, HOPE, STRENGTH, AND AS CRUCIFIED WITH CHRIST.* THESE FIVE REALITIES WERE THE UNLIMITED PRIVILEGES OF BECOMING A CHILD OF GOD.

I closed my eyes.

I felt seen. I felt enclosed. I felt protected.

Something sparked in my soul. Something blossomed. Something formed. It was as if that verb architected a whole new place within, brick by brick. Each brick became a different facet of the Guarding God operating inside me based on everything I'd ever read about God in the Bible. That day, I began to synthesize all I knew about Him and uncovered that someone in God's guarding care lives in five new ways:

A person God guards lives with *confidence, peace, hope, strength,* and *as crucified with Christ.* These five realities were the unlimited privileges of becoming a child of God. These five realities represent what Jesus offers and works into the human soul. Theologian Dallas Willard explains, "Spiritual formation for the Christian basically refers to the Spirit-driven process of forming the inner world of the human self in such a way that it becomes like the inner being of Christ himself."[1]

Our inner world can indeed become like Christ. We can find, through Jesus, maturity and stability, drawing joy from a continual source of intimacy with Him. People who know Jesus like this would have the emotional regulation and well-being I wanted but had never accessed. They would love Him and worship Him even more because they knew Him in these new ways.

I knew that I didn't live like someone who experienced Jesus' guarding and keeping care. Instead of resting in God's guarding care, I stayed trapped in a pinball machine of unstable living, ricocheting between these five toxic mindsets: condemnation, anxiety, hopelessness, weakness, and self-absorption. Even while I enjoyed months of spiritual growth and intimacy with Jesus, I felt like I backslid into a default state of instability more often than I wanted to. Could I grow up into my salvation in such a way that I could experience God's guarding care all day long? I didn't want to live such a fragile life anymore.

Instead of a *guarded* mindset, I had a *distressed* mindset.

Reading that God guarded me was like an invitation to another kind of living with a different set of opposing and triumphing mindsets. This kind of living was a decisive revolution that dethroned what kept me miserable and disconnected from Jesus, others, and even myself. In the fresh space of my soul, I learned the truth:

Jesus offers righteousness to combat condemnation and
shame (Romans 8:1).
Jesus transfers His peace to soothe anxiety (Philippians 4:7).
Jesus supplies His hope to flood light into dark despair
(Romans 15:13).
Jesus infuses His power to aid our weakness (Ephesians 1:19).
Jesus lives in us to transform a self-life into a crucified life
(Galatians 2:20).

Christ was guarding me and offering these unlimited privileges;
I needed to learn how to take up residence in my own soul with Jesus
and learn a different way to be. And it wasn't all just about *me*; the
inward work of knowing a Guarding God was about so much more
than just my own soul and my own life. Christ guarded me alongside other believers who were together manifesting God's presence.
His guarding presence was always an invitation to move more and
more outside myself to connect with others and minister to them. I
had wanted to experience what the Bible calls "the body of Christ"
(1 Corinthians 12:27), but my emotions and inner world often isolated and separated me more than connected me to others.

But Jesus was offering me a soul-makeover, a complete renovation that would heal the deepest parts of me and grow me into
maturity and deep, authentic connection with others. Jesus is also
called *Immanuel* (Isaiah 7:14 and Matthew 1:23), which means
God with us, and this renovation and subsequent maturity had everything to do with learning *how* Jesus was with me, with us.

———✳———

Before learning *how* God was guarding me, I had to understand more of *where* He was guarding me. Perhaps like me, you're

a visual learner, and picturing this abstract concept helps you grasp biblical truth. If we examine images where God's people imagined His guarding care in Scripture, we see the repetition of these images: shield, refuge, rock, tower, or fortress.[2] In Psalm 18:2, for example, we see David proclaiming his confidence in God's love and protection when he describes these images: "The Lord is my rock, my fortress and my deliverer; my God is my rock, in whom I take refuge, my shield." Picture these images in your mind: a rock, a fortress, a shield.

> JESUS INVITES US TO LIVE FROM OUR INNER BEING, AND AS DAVID DID, WE CAN PICTURE OURSELVES IN THE FORTRESS OF GOD'S GUARDING CARE IN OUR SOULS.

Over and over again throughout the Psalms, we see images of invisible structures into which these writers imaginatively placed themselves under guard by a powerful, loving, all-seeing God. But they aren't physical places. It's just like what Herman Melville wrote in *Moby Dick* when describing a setting. He claims, "It is not down in any map; true places never are."

The fortresses, shields, and refuges of God are true, but unseen places. They are spiritual images or metaphors that helped the biblical writers understand how God was guarding their souls. David wasn't literally present in any of these towers, fortresses, shields, and refuges, but in his spiritual reality, he was there. So strong was this spiritual understanding that David even proclaims in Psalm 11:1, "In the Lord I take refuge. How then can you say to me: 'Flee like a bird to your mountain'?" In other words, David tells us—"I'm already in a place of safely, so I don't need to run to another place of protection." *We don't need to run anywhere else. Jesus is our refuge.*

David, well before the coming of Christ who instructs us on His indwelling presence, understood that he was somehow dwelling in God, taking refuge there.

God's guarding presence is also *in our souls*. Does this seem strange or hard to believe? Many passages of Scripture indicate this reality as noted by 2 Corinthians 13:5, where Paul simply asks, "Do you not realize that Christ Jesus *is in you*?" We might look to Ephesians 3:17, where Paul says that Christ is dwelling "*in your hearts*" through faith." God's guarding presence is within us at this very moment if we've invited Jesus to dwell there by receiving His free gift of salvation.

This indwelling Christ that was once so hard to picture suddenly had clarity when I remembered David's dwelling places. Every biblical image of God as this external shield, tower, fortress, or refuge applies *within our very own souls* because of the indwelling Christ by the Holy Spirit. God Himself is our dwelling place, our refuge, and our fortress (Psalms 90:1; 91:2) and this happens within us. Jesus invites us to live from our inner being, and as David did, we can picture ourselves in the fortress of God's guarding care in our souls.

It now didn't matter that I was in an old apartment in a strange city. I was in a different setting in my soul—in a fortress of God's guarding care. It was like a Promised Land inside .

Maybe this is what Jesus wanted for us all along when He taught about our inner being. In one of His most powerful teaching moments—during the Feast of Tabernacles (which was the Jewish festival remembering how the Israelites lived in temporary dwellings while wandering in the wilderness)—He says something astonishing about our inner being, the dwelling place of God. We read in John 7:37–39:

On the last and greatest day of the festival, Jesus stood and said in a loud voice, "Let anyone who is thirsty come to me and drink. Whoever believes in me, as Scripture has said, rivers of living water will flow from within them." By this he meant the Spirit, whom those who believed in him were later to receive.

Jesus claims that He is "living water" and that He can flow "from within" us. These images counted as revolutionary words in a setting where Jews celebrated external dwelling places and years of wandering before entering the Promised Land of Canaan. Essentially, Jesus proclaimed a new kind of dwelling—an indwelling, and another kind of Promised Land *within*.[3]

Think of the fresh, nourishing, vibrant life of Jesus right now in our inner being. This is a new life, lived from within, that aligns us to the indwelling Christ all day long.

—⟡—

If you're anything like me, you don't always feel the fresh, nourishing, vibrant inner life because your outer life suffers. Life, for you, might feel more like a dry desert than a flowing river. You aren't alone. In 2 Corinthians 4:16 we read, "Therefore we do not lose heart. Though outwardly we are wasting away, yet inwardly we are being renewed day by day." God's guarding presence renews us, although on the outside, life might not look as abundant as we had hoped. You may agree with the idea that parts of your life are "wasting away" through such things as aging, disease, loss of loved ones, or any category of disappointments, but you might not have ever experienced "being renewed day by day."

You might be reading this and wonder how to keep reading because of some terrible thing that has happened in your life. You don't presently feel guarded in the fortress of God's loving care, and you didn't feel guarded when *that thing* happened. I pray you'll find encouragement as you read on. Besides coming to terms with my own journey of anxiety and depression as I sought to understand how God guards my soul, I encountered many scenarios of suffering Christians who nevertheless know something deeply true about Jesus that goes beyond what's happening to them physically or even in their own minds.

I felt inspired—and troubled—by their stories. How could they live from their inner beings when life was falling apart around them? What do they know about Jesus that enables this?

In one weekend alone, I met with a woman whose marriage was ending but who nevertheless knew an indescribable peace, hope, and strength from Jesus. I sat in a living room with someone who faces a lifetime of chronic pain and disease. She takes her frail body and worships Jesus facedown on the floor of her bedroom because He has been so good to her. I spent time with a grieving couple whose first child had died unexpectedly and who still came to church to worship Jesus. This was just in my own small town. The online community connects us to even more friends going through unimaginable pain. So if you aren't presently suffering, you likely know many who are. You might be wondering, "Can they worship a God who allows this kind of loss and pain?"

Yes, they can. And they *do.*

Think of Corrie ten Boom in her wonderful book *The Hiding Place* and the power and beauty of a faith that knew God's love in the starvation, pain, and humiliation of the Nazi concentration camp. Corrie describes the moment her dear sister, Betsie, died beside her. As Betsie breathed her last in the freezing sleet amid the horrors of that place, she whispered, "We must tell people what we have learned here. We must tell them that there is no pit so deep that He is not deeper still. They will listen to us, Corrie, because we have been here."[4] Later, Corrie would say, "With Jesus even in our darkest moments, the best remains and the very best is yet to be."

I also remembered the story of the great hymnist Horatio Spafford who penned the famous hymn "It Is Well with My Soul." He wrote, "When peace like a river, attendeth my way/ When sorrows like sea billows roll / Whatever my lot, Thou hast taught me to say, It is well, it is well, with my soul."

It is well with my soul.

Do you know the story of why and how Spafford wrote that line? Spafford's four daughters drowned in a shipwreck. What many people don't realize is the reason why Spafford wasn't on that ship; he sent his family on the journey across the Atlantic without him as he tended to the disaster back home, the Great Chicago Fire, that financially ruined him. When Spafford left Chicago to meet his grieving wife, the historical account states that he was inspired to write "It is well with my soul" as the ship passed the very spot where his daughters were believed to have drowned.[5] Yes, he penned this declaration in catastrophic loss. What could be worse than financial ruin, the death of his beloved daughters, and journeying to meet his grieving wife? Yet he proclaimed, "It is well with my soul," and I was beginning to think that, no matter what happened to me, I could too. And so could you.

When I thought of both Corrie ten Boom and Horatio Spafford and how, in the midst of horrific loss, they somehow knew God's guarding presence and love—that it could "be well with their souls"—I continued to ask the age old question: How? How could Paul, for example, say in Philippians 4:11 that he had "learned to be content whatever the circumstances"?

I had always wanted a God who guards my life and every external thing that concerns me. We all do. But I paused and reflected on the psalmists who wrote in the midst of danger and loss. I paused as I considered Paul writing from a Roman prison. I paused when I remembered Corrie ten Boom and Horatio Spafford. I paused, thinking of Jesus who could say, "Not as I will, but as you will" when faced with unimaginable, incomprehensible, agonizing execution on a cross (Matthew 26:39). It wasn't always well with their lives, but it was *always well with their souls.*

> BECAUSE OF THIS GUARDING GOD, WE LEARN TO DWELL IN OUR SOUL MORE THAN IN OUR LIFE'S EXTERNAL REALITIES, AND WE BECOME STRONG AND UNSHAKEABLE IN A WORLD THAT'S FALLING APART.

Knowing God guards our soul—and doesn't necessarily promise physical well-being—provides a powerful opportunity: the opportunity to live not in bitterness, anger, cynicism, and disillusionment—but to live in the righteousness, hope, peace, power, and selflessness of the gospel. After all, we know that the world we live in exists in "bondage to decay" (Romans 8:21). In many ways, we should expect disease, pain, and suffering as we live in a fallen world where sin and Satan operate.

But nothing can harm a soul God guards. Because of this Guarding God, we learn to dwell in our soul more than in our life's external realities, and we become strong and unshakeable in a world that's falling apart. God is guarding our souls and teaching us to live from our inner being instead of our external circumstances.

And we more deeply know a God who has rescued our souls and keeps us in His embrace.

We meet Jesus who guards our soul, and we worship Him. We know that God "works out everything in conformity with the purpose of his will" (Ephesians 1:11). We can say, like Paul, "What has happened to me will turn out for my deliverance" (Philippians 1:19). This soul was made to experience Jesus even in sorrow and suffering because we trust His goodness and ability to work "for the good of those who love him" (Romans 8:28) in all things. And when we cannot see how or when, we know that we have everything we need right here because Jesus is dwelling within us, closer than our own hearts.

All of these stories—the heroes of the Christian faith and the suffering ones you and I know—can be the way God shakes us up to know Him better. As I thought of Victor Hugo's words "God stirs up the soul as well as the ocean,"[6] I was stirred up. I was shaken. Hannah Whitall Smith calls this experience the "shakings of God" that disturb every false resting place of our soul so we rest in God alone, our true kingdom, our true resting place.[7]

Are you ready to connect with Jesus in a new way and receive all the benefits of His guarding care? Are you ready to let the truths of God's guarding presence work like Aspen seedlings turning into far-spreading, indestructible roots that stretch out to overtake your emotions and experiences? As we study the aspects of our Guarding God, we're invited to become "strong in the Lord" (Ephesians 6:10) and like the person described in James 1:4 who is "mature and complete, not lacking anything."

You can know God like this—the way the psalmists knew Him, the way Paul knew Him, and the way both so many heroes of the faith and ordinary Christians seem to know Him. They learned the secret of living from *their inner being* and not from external circumstances. We, too, can dwell in His guarding presence in our inner being. Brother Lawrence, the Carmelite monk, wrote in the seventeenth century this reflection:

> I cannot imagine how religious persons can live satisfied without the practice of the presence of God. For my part, I keep myself retired with Him in the depth of centre of my soul as much as I can; and while I am so with Him, I fear nothing; but the least turning from Him is insupportable.[8]

Wouldn't you love to retire with Him in the depth and center of your soul all day long? We can, right now, cultivate an unshakable inner world. In this unseen but true place, we meet our Guarding God who rescues us and keeps us in His grip.

STIRRING OUR SOULS

1. Read Ephesians 3:14–21. Which words in the passage make you most eager to know Jesus better? Which parts of this passage have you personally experienced? Which parts do you pray you could experience more in your life?

2. How have you been taught to think about your "inner being"? When you imagine "rivers of living water flowing from within" you (John 7:37–39), what comes to mind?

3. Write down one or two examples from your own life when something terrible happened that "turned out for your deliverance" or "for your good" (see Philippians 1:19; Romans 8:28). Or have you experienced a moment where you could say, like Betsie ten Boom, "There is no pit so deep that He is not deeper still"?

4. In your own words, write down what you think Paul knew about God that allowed him to be "content in any and every situation" (Philippians 4:12).

———⟋⟍———

CHAPTER 2

RESCUED AND KEPT

Guard my life and rescue me.
—KING DAVID, PSALM 25:20

*Has not God given Christ His Almighty Son to be the Keeper
of every believer, to make Christ an ever-present reality, and
to impart and communicate to us all that we have in Christ?
God has given us His Son, and God has given His Spirit.
How it is that believers do not live up to their privileges?*

—SOUTH AFRICAN PREACHER ANDREW MURRAY

Thinking of the God who guards, do you wonder *why* we're being guarded?

Without His guarding care, would we live in danger and distress? Apart from Jesus, what would happen to us? The question "Why do I need God's guarding care?" adds a deeper level of inquiry into that word. And *guard* takes on greater urgency; it's an alarming word. It's a word that means we're in danger apart from God.

Do we believe this? Do we feel it in our souls? Or do we recite the gospel message to ourselves as if it really didn't matter one way or the other?

We can sing gentle praise songs and read innocuous Bible

stories when we're dealing with something more terrible and more deadly than we can describe. We're dealing with words that have been so overused they feel emptied of their power; words like "sin" and "Satan" and "evil" and "death."

These are not pleasant words. But they are words that make the word "guarded" come to life for us.

Through the pages of Scripture, we meet a God who rescues and keeps us in His guarding care. In fact, He's continually drawing us closer and closer to Him. I hope as you read this book, you feel drawn closer into Jesus' care. Yes, to know Jesus as our guarding and keeping God we need to understand more fully what it is we're rescued *from*.

If you wonder why we need rescue, you aren't alone. Most people misunderstand the gravity and desperation of what's happening to our souls apart from Jesus. Scripture teaches that we are enslaved to Satan, sin, and even ourselves.

Even as a child, I understood that this world had the same problem I did; it was a problem called "sin," and it was the things we think, say, and do that don't please God.

Our younger daughter, Kate, now a fifth grader, tells me her own words for sin: Not having a good heart sometimes; not being perfect; not doing what God would do in every situation. I was her same age when I felt this sickness in my soul. God was holy; He was absolutely perfect and could only allow holy things in His presence. How could I enter His presence? How could I find holiness?

I wanted God to rescue me from sin, cleanse me, and take me into His keeping care, covering me completely with His own holiness. But I had to admit my need for this cleansing. I had to admit I was a sinner, separated from God and unable to meet the standards for holiness. I had to be honest about the state of my soul.

When Kate was four years old, she sat with me as I frosted holiday cookies. As I left the kitchen to fold the laundry, I said, "Kate, do not touch the cookies as the frosting hardens. I'm going into the bedroom. Do not touch the cookies."

As I folded the laundry, the kitchen seemed strangely quiet.

"Kate," I called out as I folded another shirt, "are you touching the cookies?"

After a long pause, I heard her little voice:

"No." Another pause. "But they are touching me."

Kate could not admit her fault. Like most of us, she equivocated, making an excuse, even changing reality (they are touching me!) to suit her own desires in that situation. She could not escape the need to do what she wants and when she wants, no matter the rules.

While the cookie story makes our family laugh all these years later, it also serves as an illustration of my own heart's tendencies. I'm a sinner who must touch the frosting. I'm Eve who must eat the fruit. My soul wants its own way, no matter what. But what if this independence represents, not freedom, but enslavement? Jesus made this amazing statement: "The Son of Man did not come to be served, but to serve, and to give his life as a ransom for many" (Matthew 20:28). His death is a *ransom* paid for us. One pays a ransom for a precious person who has been kidnapped and taken as a slave. You may ask, then, from what do we need to be ransomed? Who or what holds us captive?

Mostly, I felt captive to myself before I truly understood the gospel and my need for salvation. I wanted to be good, but I was not. I would record lines from great writers who seemed to articulate what I knew was true of my own wayward soul. From *Robinson Crusoe*, I wrote down Daniel Defoe's idea of our inner life having a "secret overruling decree that hurries us on to be the instruments of our own destruction."[1] John Steinbeck in *East of Eden*, wrote the following: "We are capable of many things in all directions, of great virtues and great sins. And who in his mind has not probed the black water? Maybe we all have in us a secret pond where evil and ugly things germinate and grow strong."[2] I had a secret pond of desire and gluttony and self-absorption.

It didn't matter that I *wanted* to know God and to please Him, because I simply *couldn't*. I had no self-control and no power to change my desires. Can you relate to this problem?

The writer of Hebrews explains that "Christ . . . has died as a ransom to set them free from the sins committed under the first covenant" (Hebrews 9:15). In other words, we are lawbreakers, sinners unable to fulfill God's righteous requirements. The Greek language brings clarity when we learn that "ransom" means the price offered to buy someone out of slavery as well as the price paid to liberate someone from the misery and penalty of sin.

Maybe we don't feel the misery and penalty of sin now, but we will. Scripture tells us that sin brings trouble and distress and ultimately death. It brings judgment and eternal separation from God, described in sobering terms in Scripture. Many people have such a hard time considering future separation from God or a state of "hell" that they hardly talk about it because it's too scary or difficult. Whether or not I can conceptualize or understand this separation from God, I know that without Jesus, we're already experiencing, in part, desperation and destruction.

We are indeed prisoners who desperately need rescue right now.

Scripture clarifies the true story of the human soul throughout its pages. For example, when Paul writes of his battle with sin, he claims in Romans 7:14–25:

I am unspiritual, sold as a slave to sin. I do not understand what I do. For what I want to do I do not do, but what I hate I do . . . As it is, it is no longer I myself who do it, but it is sin living in me. For I know that good itself does not dwell in me, that is, in my sinful nature. For I have the desire to do what is good, but I cannot carry it out. . . . What a wretched man I am! Who will rescue me from this body of death? Thanks be to God—through Jesus Christ our Lord!

Paul explains that he is unspiritual, enslaved, and bound by a sinful nature. When he writes, "nothing good lives in me," I related deeply. I was, and often still am, imprisoned to appetites, moods, desires, and greed. I'm jealous, petty, and easily angered. I demand my own way and place myself at the center of the universe. Who can save me? Like me, have you, or do you, feel the captivity in your own being? Whether or not we are emotionally aware of any kind of captivity or bitterness, we at least know that we're not able to be the people we want to be. We're not able to respond to others as we wish—with patience and love—and instead act selfishly. Sometimes we feel trapped by desires we must fight. I spent years making bad choices, hurting others, and obeying every impulse. Can you relate? Who can save us?

You may not fully understand your own soul's plight—or perhaps you do, and are ready for a fuller understanding—but it's written throughout the Bible and it accounts for the suffering we feel both in ourselves and see in the world. Even if you don't feel bound to Satan, we're told in Scripture that we are captives, essentially, to our sin nature. Andrew Murray explains it like this:

Self is the great curse, whether in its relation to God, or to our fellow-men in general, or to fellow-Christians, thinking of ourselves and seeking our own. Self is our greatest curse. But praise God, Christ came to redeem us from self.[3]

Each of us is a captive—to sin and to even ourselves—who needs a rescuer. This is the plain truth. We each need rescue from coming judgment, from Satan's accusations against us, and from our own sin nature. We need rescue from the power of sin that works destruction within us.

This is a profoundly different way of thinking about ourselves than what the culture teaches. Most contemporary therapeutic practices and self-help books, for example, offer coping mechanisms and strategies for better living, but they do not provide the soul transformation we need inside where we exchange our sinful nature to become a "new creation" in Christ (2 Corinthians 5:17). We cannot meditate our way out of the reality of our nature that lives in opposition to God. We are enslaved, and wishful thinking, deep breathing, and guided imagery cannot release us. Even though we can improve the quality of our lives through exercise, weight loss, new jobs, new friends, or new houses, these elements can never release us from what we most need: rescue from sin's power.

Nothing we can do—no program, no spiritual practice, no technique—and nothing we can buy or experience can do what only Jesus can do for us. Only Jesus can bring new life to an imprisoned soul. Have you felt this new life inside of you? Have you ever experienced being set free from the power of sin? Have you met Jesus as your rescuer?

I remember the moment I sat in a coffee shop in Blacksburg, Virginia, with my big sister, Melissa, who was a junior at Virginia

Tech. She had driven all the way to the University of Virginia to rescue me for the weekend. I was a freshman trying to find meaning and satisfaction in everything other than Jesus, and I was making a mess of my life. Perhaps you're reading this and can relate. That weekend included me crying in the backseat of my sister's Honda as she played Christian music (Rich Mullins's "Hold Me, Jesus") and talked to me about God's love. Imagine us then sitting in Mill Mountain coffee shop, with the hiss of espresso machines, the clinking of coffee mugs, and the hum of a hundred lively conversations. Imagine a young woman crying over all the wrong choices and all the ways she needed rescue as her big sister listened. Imagine the crying girl saying, "I just know that if Jesus were here, He wouldn't want me. He wouldn't choose me." But Jesus *did* want her. Jesus *did* choose her for His own. He was right there, ready to rescue.

> WHEN WE BELIEVE IN JESUS, HE RESCUES US FROM DARKNESS. HE TRANSFERS US TO A NEW KINGDOM. WE CROSS OVER TO LIFE.

And then imagine a girl with a new Bible, a prayer of surrender to Jesus, and God who swooped in and rescued her from *herself.*

Jesus Christ renews our inner being through the Holy Spirit. Apart from Jesus, we live in spiritual darkness, and we need a Savior to bring us into another kingdom. Colossians 1:13–14 states it so beautifully and powerfully: "For he has rescued us from the dominion of darkness and brought us in the kingdom of the Son he loves, in whom we have redemption, the forgiveness of sins."

We have been rescued from one kingdom and brought into another. Jesus Himself explains this transfer when He says in John 5:24, "Whoever hears my word and believes him who sent me has eternal life and will not be judged but has crossed over from death to life." To have crossed over from death to life, to have left a dominion of darkness, to have been brought into a new kingdom because of Jesus makes my heart explode in worship.

I cannot fathom it, really. It feels like a remedy for a disease I didn't always realize I had, like someone on the brink of death, saved despite not realizing the full danger. But when I think carefully about it, I know I've been acquainted with the darkness, with the sickening weight of sin, and with the internal existential crisis that something isn't right with me and the whole world. When I read Scriptures that discuss the spiritual reality of demonic forces, I realize that so much more is happening around us than we can perceive. We need protection. We need a Guarding God.

This God rescues us from darkness. He transfers us to a new kingdom. We cross over to life.

Colossians 2:13 says it simply: "You were dead in your sins . . . God made you alive with Christ."

Now we are living a glorious new life—a totally different kind of living because we are "alive with Christ." Our souls are alive to Jesus and growing into greater and greater likeness to Jesus. We were dead but now *alive*. When Jesus offers His life for us, we take on His resurrected life and become new creations. This new life in Christ happens by the indwelling spirit of God.

Maybe the reason so many heroes of the faith can say, "It is well with my soul" is that they remember, most of all, that they have been *rescued*. They remember that once, they were guarded by sin, enslaved to sin, and barricaded by the dominion of darkness on all sides. And now, when they receive Christ, they are guarded by righteousness, peace, power, hope, and are hidden in Christ in this new barricaded fortress of God's love.

Perhaps God as our Rescuer is what the strongest, most vibrant Christians know and remember most about Jesus when they think of Him. I recently emailed the son of the late Dr. Bill Bright—the founder of Campus Crusade for Christ International (CRU)—to find out more about what Donald Miller wrote about Dr. Bright in *Blue Like Jazz*. The story goes that when someone asked Dr. Bright what Jesus meant to him, "Dr. Bright could not answer the question. . . . He just started to cry. He sat there in his big chair behind his big desk and wept."[4]

WHAT DOES JESUS MEAN TO YOU? IF YOU DON'T YET KNOW JESUS, WHAT IS IT THAT YOU'VE HEARD ABOUT HIM THAT DRAWS YOU TO HIM?

Dr. Bright's son told me that this "was an accurate description of my dad's heart."[5] When I picture Dr. Bright crying at his desk at the mere mention of the name of Jesus, I feel my throat go tight and have an ache in my heart.

I asked my husband, "What does Jesus mean to you?" and he too couldn't speak for a moment. I asked my daughters, and the older one said, "Mom, I want to know Jesus like Dr. Bright did. I want to cry at the mention of His name because I love Him so much and He loves me."

I asked a group of three hundred women at a conference, "What does Jesus mean to you? Turn to the woman beside you," I instructed, "and just use a few words to describe your answer. And if you don't yet know Jesus, what is it that you've heard about Him that draws you to Him?" I stood on the stage, waiting to hear all the lively conversation, but instead I saw the entire front row of women's faces streaming with tears.

I didn't hear words; I saw tears. I wonder if, at that moment, they knew Jesus as their rescuer, and it was too beautiful and powerful for words.

It's clear: We've been rescued.

From the power of sin.

From condemnation.

From spiritual death.

From ourselves.

We've been brought into a relationship with God and now we are kept there. He will never leave us. We've been adopted into God's family (John 1:12), given new life (2 Corinthians 5:17), and promised eternal life (1 John 5:11–13). God keeps us in His hands forever.

This I now needed to understand: I was rescued and now *kept*.

—␣␣—

I was twenty-two-years old—now five years after the Mill Mountain coffee shop conversation with my sister—and sitting in the student union of the University of Michigan. I was munching on a hamburger and fries and guzzling coffee to survive the upcoming afternoon that included hosting student office hours, leading a discussion section on Shakespeare's *Merchant of Venice*, and attending a graduate seminar on critical theory, when a Cru staff woman engaged me in conversation and shared John 10:28. Together, with the Bible opened, we read Jesus' statement: "I give them eternal life . . . no one will snatch them out of my hand. My Father, who has given them to me, is greater than all; no one can snatch them out of my Father's hand." We talked about how Jesus kept me safely in His grip. *He loved me and kept me.*

But despite having accepted Jesus several years before, I didn't feel loved or accepted or kept by Him. I felt I had sinned too much, been too much of a disappointment, and was not worthy of Jesus. Had God rejected me? Was I really still His child? I falsely believed that, as soon as I sinned in any way—in dating relationships, at parties, even through my speech and attitudes—God turned His back on me and I would have to start all over again to win His approval and favor. Even if I confessed my sin, I still felt condemned, unworthy, and disconnected from Jesus. I knew He could rescue me from sin, but I didn't know anything about His *keeping of me*.

That day in the student union, the staff member and I considered together that *Jesus was keeping me*. I was held tightly in His hand, and nothing—not even myself—could remove me from that grip. We discussed the permanence of such statements like this from Ephesians 1:13–14: "And you also were included in Christ when you heard the message of truth, the gospel of your salvation. When you believed, you were marked in him with a seal, the promised Holy Spirit, who is a deposit guaranteeing our inheritance." Since I had already received Christ some time before, I was marked and sealed, included and guaranteed. Now I had to teach my soul to believe the truth that God kept me, no matter what was happening in my own life, in my own sin, and in my own mind. *God was keeping me in His hands.*

I always wondered about Jesus' statement that nothing could snatch His sheep out of His hand. The staff woman took her wedding ring off and hid it in her palm, and then made a fist around it. "Try to remove the ring," she said. When I went to try to pry her fingers open, she said, "Wait, I'm going to put another hand over my first, doubling protecting that ring." She told me that I was like that wedding ring inside Jesus' hand that was enclosed doubly by the Father's hands.

I was doubly guarded, doubly kept.

This idea of "double keeping" struck me powerfully when I read Psalm 140:4 where David repeats the cry for God to keep him. He uses two different forms of the verb "to keep." He says, for example: "Keep me, O Lord, from the hands of the wicked; preserve me" (NASB). The first verb, keep, is *shamar*, which we know means to carefully protect, observe, and guard. The next verb, preserve (often translated "keep"), is *natsar*, which means to barricade and keep close. One Hebrew scholar explains that *natsar* is a stronger form of keeping than *shamar*. It suggests a watching, keeping, and defending that are more intense than *shamar*. It's a greater degree of keeping.[6]

> "I'M KEPT BY HIM! I THOUGHT I WAS REJECTED, BUT MY SIN DOESN'T END MY RELATIONSHIP WITH JESUS! IT JUST TEMPORARILY CHANGES MY INTIMACY WITH HIM!"

This God who "keeps me twice" created a new security in me. That day in the student union, my mentor and I drew a diagram to explain the keeping power of Jesus. It was a solid circle with Jesus and me in the middle. Nothing could get me out of that circle. Inside the solid circle, however, was a dotted line—an inner circle—that I could enter and leave. This permeable circle represented my intimacy or fellowship with Jesus that could indeed change based on sin in my life, but at no time was my *permanent relationship* with God threatened. I was His daughter, and just as a mother cannot change the fact of her biological relationship to her daughter, I was permanently fixed in the family of God.

I ran from the student union in the snow—black coat swinging and boots sloshing and sliding on the ice—to return to my office hours in the English department. I felt like I might burst with this incredible information about Jesus. I couldn't contain myself. I wanted to shout: "I'm kept by Him! I thought I was rejected, but my sin doesn't end my relationship with Jesus! It just temporarily changes my intimacy with Him!"

This news I shared indiscriminately with other PhD colleagues and students just for the pure joy of what I had learned and now believed. "Can I tell you what I just learned about Jesus?" I asked, and drew the diagram and talked about this keeping God that whole afternoon. As a PhD student in English literature, I was supposed to be standoffish and snobby, tucked away with poetry and scholarly jargon, but instead, I was twirling in my office amid the dusty anthologies of Wordsworth, Coleridge, and Browning and knowing that the "sense sublime" those poets wrote about was happening to me right now because of Jesus.

It didn't matter that I had a terrible haircut, a recent breakup, and a professor who thought I wasn't smart enough to survive his seminar. Why did any of it matter when Jesus kept me in His grip? What greater thing could I ever learn in my whole life that could surpass the knowledge that I was kept by Jesus?

I understood what Andrew Murray wrote:

What is kept? You are kept. How much of you? The whole being. Does God keep one part of you and not another? No. Some people have an idea that this is a sort of vague general keeping, and that God will keep them in such a way that when they die they will get to Heaven. But they do not apply that word kept to everything in their being and nature. And yet this is what God wants.[7]

We are kept. Our whole being is kept.

As I continue to meditate on God's keeping presence in my life, I turn to the beautiful Psalm 121 where God is called "The Keeper of Israel."

> I lift up my eyes to the mountains—
>> where does my help come from?
> My help comes from the Lord,
>> the Maker of heaven and earth.
> He will not let your foot slip—
>> he who watches over you will not slumber;
> indeed, he who watches over Israel
>> will neither slumber nor sleep.
> The Lord watches over you—
>> the Lord is your shade at your right hand;
> the sun will not harm you by day,
>> nor the moon by night.
> The Lord will keep you from all harm—
>> he will watch over your life;
> the Lord will watch over your coming and going
>> both now and forevermore.

Six different times, we see that precious verb *shamar*. He won't let us slip; He watches over us; we are kept from harm. Our Guarding God is a keeping God, and we can rest forever in the truth of it. The preacher Charles Spurgeon's commentary on this psalm brings such comfort to my soul. He writes:

> If the soul be kept all is kept . . . God is the sole keeper of the soul. Our soul is kept from the dominion of sin, the infection

of error, the crush of despondency, the puffing up of pride; kept from the world, the flesh, and the devil; kept for holier and greater things; kept in the love of God; kept unto the eternal kingdom and glory. What can harm a soul that is kept of the Lord?[8]

All is kept. All is well. What can harm a soul that is kept of the Lord?

STIRRING OUR SOULS

1. How would you answer this question: What does Jesus mean to you?

2. From what does Jesus rescue us? List everything you've personally been rescued from. In other words, apart from Jesus' rescuing power, what do you think your life would be like?

3. Read John 10:25–30. Why is it so hard to believe that "nothing can snatch us out of his hand"?

4. In Psalm 121, we see our guarding and keeping God at work. What does it mean for you at this moment that God will "watch over your life"?

CHAPTER 3

—୬୬—

REFRESHING THE MEMORY

The key, then, to loving God is to see Jesus, to hold him
before the mind with as much fullness and clarity as possible.

—DALLAS WILLARD

So I will always remind you of these things, even though
you know them and are firmly established in the truth
you now have. I think it is right to refresh your memory.

—THE APOSTLE PETER IN 2 PETER 1:12–13

Dallas Willard claimed the key to loving God is to "hold [Jesus] before the mind with as much fullness and clarity as possible."[1]

Several years ago, my love for God—and my daily experience of Him—flamed within me because of how I pictured a single word in Scripture that helped me hold Jesus in my mind. I had read Ephesians 2:6 where Paul writes that "God raised us up with Christ and seated us with him in the heavenly realms in Christ Jesus." That word, seated, gave me a picture I could see in my mind about what was happening to me in the spiritual realm. When I recognized I was seated with Christ at a table, I could remember my identity.

Yes, I pictured a seat. I remembered Jesus because of my seat at the table.

When I wrote *Seated with Christ: Living Freely in a Culture of Comparison*, I enjoyed several radio interviews in the first months of publication. Many of the radio hosts were interested in the same question:

"How? How can the word *seated* change someone like this? How do you apply it each day?"

I probably sounded simple and not very theologically sophisticated. "Well, I just remember it each morning. I refresh my memory with the picture of my seat at the table." I didn't know how else to explain it other than the Holy Spirit used the image of that verb in Ephesians. I could remember the image of a seat at the table and go about my day as a new person.

The transformative, powerful memory technique was to *recognize what was happening* in the heavenly realms according to what the verse said. In this case, Paul writes that we are "seated with Christ in the heavenly realms," so I painted the picture in my soul of a grand, round table like the Round Table from the Arthurian legend. I positioned myself in my seat with as much detail as I could, knowing Jesus was beside me. There at the table, I began to recall verbs regarding how seated people live. I said to my soul, "I'm seated and adoring, accessing, and abiding." I used images and words I could remember (it was easier for me if each word began with the same letter, and I chose "a") to train my mind to recall this data throughout every single day. It was a strategy that ancient philosophers and now modern educators have always utilized: picturing and repeating words to remember.

Cleaning dishes, I was seated at a royal table and accessing the riches of God.

Giving a grammar lesson on campus, I was seated at the greatest table with the greatest King and abiding to produce the fruit He ordained for me.

When I felt fat and ugly, I was seated and adoring, radiating the beauty of Christ.

I recalled the image and the "a" words and *I remembered who I was in Christ.*

It wasn't strange, unbiblical, or useless. It wasn't a form of New Age mysticism or anything based in the power of the images themselves. Instead, recognizing what Scripture was saying about Jesus —using all the senses to create mental images—was something Jesus Himself modeled for His followers because these pictures brought people back to biblical truth and connected them again to their own souls. The images were a form of education and memory.

As the greatest teacher, Jesus used ordinary objects to help His followers refresh their memories and understand more about Him. For example, when He compares Himself to bread (John 6:35), light (John 8:12), a gate (John 10:7), a shepherd (John 10:11), and a vine (John 15:1), His listeners had *mental images triggered by everyday objects* to recall crucial information about Him.

Those early followers of Jesus who were just learning to live their new lives in Christ had a whole collection of objects to remember Jesus. Perhaps if, when they smelled the delicious, grainy aroma of baking loaves and when they ate that fresh *bread*, they remembered that Jesus satisfied their spiritual hunger and gave His life for them. Or possibly when they walked through a *gate*, they remembered their Savior who invites entrance into eternal life. Maybe when they saw *shepherds with their sheep* in the Judean countryside, they remembered Jesus as their Good Shepherd who offered safe pasture and abundant life. And, of course, when they saw the *grapevines* growing throughout the region where Jesus taught, they

IF IT IS THE SOUL THAT IS RUNNING OUR LIVES AND ORGANIZING EVERYTHING ABOUT US, THEN UNDERSTANDING WHAT IS HAPPENING WITHIN THE SOUL TAKES ON VITAL IMPORTANCE.

recalled abiding with their Savior and the abundant fruit their lives would bear for the kingdom. I wonder if, with each sip of wine, they recalled His shed blood. By using images like this, Jesus modeled how His listeners could bring spiritual truth to their minds.

It's clear that Paul instructs this form of memory when he says to picture our "seat" in the heavenly realms and to visualize ourselves putting on the "armor of God," even though both statements are entirely figurative and imaginative. We cannot see them; they exist in our mind and connect us to spiritual truths. Jesus and Paul both did what modern researchers say work best: "Complex data, when presented by a single image can be quickly absorbed by the human mind. Especially when the data is abstract . . . visualization reinforces human cognition."[2]

Recognizing my seat in the heavenly realms changed everything, so now I wondered what to picture regarding God's guarding presence in my soul. I desperately need to refresh my memory each new day because as each new morning dawns, I fall back to the default state of my flesh and sinful nature.

I forget that God guards me, that I'm rescued and kept.

Why can't I remember—in a meaningful and applicable way— that I'm guarded by Jesus, having been rescued by Him, and now I'm kept tightly in His grip? I feel like those movie characters with amnesia who need to reconstruct their identity each new day with the help of notes and photographs. As I read Willard's comments on the soul, I find more urgency in understanding, and keeping attuned to, what's happening in my soul. He writes:

> What is running your life at any given moment is your soul. Not external circumstances, not your thoughts, not your intentions, not even your feelings, but your soul. The soul is that aspect of your whole being that correlates, integrates, and enlivens everything going on in the various dimensions of the self.[3]

If it is the soul that is running our lives and organizing everything about us, then understanding what is happening within the soul, accurately and memorably, takes on vital importance. The soul, according to Willard, "integrates and enlivens everything going on" in us. So I insist to myself that I'm guarded, rescued, and kept by Jesus. I know this.

But knowing isn't the problem.
Remembering is the problem.
Calling to mind is the problem.
Accessing this knowledge is the problem.

We read and forget. We go to church and forget. We attend conferences, read books, listen to worship songs, and then we forget. Many of us don't know how to live daily in the reality of Jesus shaping within us an unshakable, steadfast soul; we struggle to live in a consistent state of victory so promised in Scripture.

THIS GUARDED SOUL, SO CAREFULLY INDWELT AND TENDED BY JESUS, IS A FORTRESS OF TRUTH WE ACCESS DESPITE ANY PHYSICAL CIRCUMSTANCES OR EMOTIONAL INSTABILITY.

I needed some way to daily remember the guarding presence of Christ inside of me so each new morning, I could say, like David in Psalm 103:1, "Praise the Lord, my soul; all my inmost being, praise his holy name." Day by day, I could know that I was indeed storm-tossed by ugly moods and unpredictable circumstances, but in my inner being, I was in the guarding presence of Christ.

This guarded soul, so carefully indwelt and tended by Jesus, is a fortress of truth we access despite any physical circumstances or emotional instability. In this fortress, we are guarded by Christ's righteousness, peace, hope, power, and His crucified life. We are hidden in Him right now and He is living through us.

When we forget this reality, we fall back into the default modes of condemnation, anxiety, hopelessness, weakness, and self-absorption. We need a different narrative than this. We need to want to "put on the new self" each day. Paul, in Colossians 3:10, discusses how we must set our minds upon Jesus and "put on the new self, which is being renewed in knowledge in the image of its Creator." Let's say, like David in Psalm 16:8: "I keep my eyes always on the Lord."

Why is this so hard? Biblical writers repeatedly tell us to call to mind, to remember the Lord, to hope in God all day long; but consider the challenges a modern audience faces to such commands. I once memorized the command in Joshua 1:8: "Keep this Book of the Law always on your lips; meditate on it day and night, so that you may be careful to do everything written in it. Then you will be prosperous and successful." But, in reality, not only could I not keep God's word always on my lips, I could not imagine what it would be like to "meditate on it day and night."

In ancient times, God's people *remembered*. Their whole way of life was centered on remembering God. God even trained them how to do so. When God speaks to Moses as recorded in Numbers 15:38–39, He says:

Speak to the Israelites and say to them: "Throughout the generations to come you are to make tassels on the corners of your garments, with a blue cord on each tassel. You will have these tassels to look at and so you will remember all the commands of the Lord, that you may obey them."

The tassels were physical, visual cues to remind the Israelites about God's commandments. They would look at the tassels and remember. I suddenly wanted tassels everywhere, but the only ones I could picture were the tassels on Magic Carpet from Disney's *Aladdin* when the genie says, "Yo, Rug Man! Haven't seen you in a few millennia. Slip me some tassel."[4] Admittedly tassels wouldn't work for most of us today, but still, memory was vital to the Israelites; God gave further memory-enhancing instructions in Deuteronomy 6:6–9:

These commandments that I give you today are to be on your hearts. Impress them on your children. Talk about them when you sit at home and when you walk along the road, when you lie down and when you get up. Tie them as symbols on your hands and bind them on your foreheads. Write them on the doorframes of your houses and on your gates.

God taught the Israelites to have symbols and written reminders—even on their bodies—to remember His commands.

Ivan Marcus, a professor of Jewish history from Yale, describes a medieval Jewish ritual designed to impart to children the importance of knowing, treasuring, internalizing, and recalling God's Word. Marcus describes how young Jewish boys participated in a special ritual around the age of five. The young boy arrived at the rabbi's home where the teacher presented him with a tablet inscribed with the Hebrew alphabet. The teacher would then smear honey on the tablet and let the young boy lick the honey off the tablet. Just then, "cakes on which biblical verses have been written are brought in."[5] The teacher proceeded to read the words on the cakes, and the boy would then eat them. During this ritual, the boy enjoys delicacies that enact the idea that God's Word is "as sweet as honey" from Ezekiel 3:1–3. Licking the honey off of the tablet also points to Psalm 119:103 where the priest writes: "How sweet are your words to my taste, sweeter than honey to my mouth!" And as the boy eats the cakes with Bible verses on them, it embodies what Jeremiah claims: "When your words came, I ate them; they were my joy and my heart's delight" (Jeremiah 15:16).[6]

We need to treasure God's Word like this—the way the ancient Jewish families did—and know how vital God's Word is to everything about our lives. We need to know it and recall it for the reasons below and more. We need to internalize it because God's Word:

> awakens and builds faith (Romans 10:17)
> creates new life in our souls (1 Peter 1:23–25)
> gives hope (Romans 15:13)
> frees us (John 8:32)
> guides us (Psalm 119:105)
> matures us (Hebrews 5:13–14)
> delights us (Psalm 119:35)
> teaches us God's promises (Psalm 119:140)
> arms us against enemy attack (Ephesians 6:17;
>   Matthew 4:3–4)
> prospers us (Psalm 1:2–3)

familiarizes us with God's voice (John 14:26)

strengthens and comforts us in suffering (Psalm 119:28)

trains and corrects us (2 Timothy 3:16–17)

sanctifies and cleanses us (Ephesians 5:26)

fills us with joy and delight (Jeremiah 15:16)

invites us to worship the Lord (Deuteronomy 17:19)

dwells in us richly (Colossians 3:16)

penetrates our hearts and minds (Hebrews 4:12)

turns our eyes from worthless things (Psalm 119:37)

keeps us from temptation (Psalm 119:11)

contains no errors (2 Samuel 22:31)

and most importantly, God's Word leads us to Jesus Christ (1 John 5:13)

We cannot deny how important it is that God's people know His words. Yet what's on my heart each day has much more to do with social media, the news, and worries and wants than my recalling of God's words. I think about caffeine and breakfast more than God's Word. I think about my own stress and agenda. Why can't I remember what God is doing in my soul like I can remember to set the coffee maker and who I'm meeting for lunch?

I wanted a well-trained memory, so vital for obeying God's command to "not forget." In Deuteronomy 4:9, we read God's clear instruction: "Only be careful, and watch yourselves closely so that you do not forget the things your eyes have seen or let them fade from your heart as long as you live. Teach them to your children and to their children after them."

Studying the number of times Jews were told to remember and not forget reveals that memory mattered deeply in ancient Jewish life. In the psalms, we have these two beautiful verses when David says, "Praise the Lord, my soul, and forget not all his benefits" and "I will never forget your precepts, for by them you have preserved my life" (103:2; 119:93). David hoped in God all day long and claims that he always had the Lord on his mind (Psalm 16:8). I wanted to be more like David, and I wanted to obey the command in 1 Chronicles 16:11 (NASB) to "Seek the Lord and His strength; seek His face *continually*."

The writers of the Bible knew the importance of *continually* keeping the Lord in our awareness by remembering Him throughout the day.

In this digital age, bringing data to the forefront of our minds is not as easy as it once was. Researchers tell us that young adults spend 85 percent of their day connected to digital devices, and they outsource their memory to their phones, laptops, or tablets. They don't know information; they mainly know how to *access* information, and this keeps data one step removed from their minds.[7] Further, "The Internet has become a primary form of external or transactive memory, where information is stored collectively outside ourselves," and, as a result, people "remember less by knowing information than by knowing where the information can be found."[8]

This is like saying we have all the food we need because it's in the grocery store. Well, how does that help when we're hungry, and how does knowing it's there bring any kind of nutrients to our body? I realized that if I roll out of bed and head to the bathroom, reluctant to face the day because of exhaustion, anxiety, or a bad mood, I don't need information about Jesus in the memory of the hard drive—I need it this moment in my mind.

I knew that if I were to live in the truth of being guarded by Christ each day, I needed to enhance and improve my memory. I wasn't going to wear tassels and write Bible verses on my forehead and doors (although I could), but I was going to pray that God would teach me how to "call to mind" the truth of His guarding presence each day. I knew I wanted *visual cues and memorable words* to help me remember things about Jesus. I wanted a rich storehouse of truth for the Holy Spirit to use all day long.

As I set about compiling everything I wanted to remember about Jesus, I continued to wonder how to best speak and teach on both *Seated with Christ* and *Guarded by Christ*. Around that time, my husband and I began watching the BBC series *Sherlock*. During the episode "The Hounds of Baskerville," Sherlock uses his "mind palace" technique to recall critical data that he knows is there but cannot access otherwise. In the episode, Sherlock tells Watson, "Get out. I need to go to my mind palace."

Watson explains, "It's a memory technique, a sort of mental map. You plot a map with a location. It doesn't have to be a real place, and then you deposit memories there so that theoretically, you can never forget anything. All you have to do is find your way back to it."[9] While the "mind palace" or "memory palace" is never mentioned specifically in the original *Adventures of Sherlock Holmes*, Arthur Conan Doyle does explain that Sherlock has a "brain attic." He writes, "I consider that a man's brain originally is like a little empty attic, and you have to stock it with such furniture as you choose."[10] As Holmes explains to Watson in Doyle's chapter:

A fool takes in all the lumber of every sort that he comes across, so that the knowledge which might be useful to him gets crowded out, or at best is jumbled up with a lot of other things, so that he has a difficulty in laying his hands upon it. Now the skillful workman is very careful indeed as to what he takes into his brain-attic.[11]

I didn't want to live like a fool. I wanted, like Sherlock, to carefully fill my mind and avoid the jumble Doyle describes. As I thought about Sherlock Holmes—the brain attic, the mind palace, my own history as an educator, and parenting of children in a digital age—I wondered about our ability to recall critical data that we need, especially in moments of distress. Like the Arthurian Round Table that I call forth in my mind every day to remember I'm seated with Christ (and I really do this every day; I'm doing it right now), might I recognize the fortress and refuge of God—where He is dwelling within me—as a place in my soul where I'm guarded at all times by several key things? And what if, like Sherlock and others who know how to retrieve information quickly by stocking a location with objects that help them recall facts, I could associate certain biblical truths about my soul with objects?

> LIKE THE BIBLICAL WRITERS, WE CAN INHABIT THE UNSEEN PLACE THAT GOD HAS BUILT IN OUR SOULS.

I could build a soul fortress, or, as my friend Hannah says, "a soul palace" like Sherlock's mind palace. C. S. Lewis preferred to call our souls "God's palace,"[12] and St. Teresa described this divine habitation of God in our souls as a mansion. She wrote, "In the centre of the soul there is a mansion reserved for God Himself."[13] Whatever you prefer to call this place in your soul, you are building an unshakable building, forged from a rich interiority of knowing God's Word.

As you continue on with each chapter, you'll find the images I choose to place in this soul fortress to recall the truth about Jesus and certain Bible verses each day. You may want to choose different images. These images, coupled with alliterative tools, work to build a moment-by-moment apparatus to keep the presence of Christ and His work in my mind and heart no matter what's going on externally. Each image and alliteration cues the passage of Scripture that transforms and renews my mind.

So when a radio host asks me how the verb "guarded" has changed me, I say how. It's because I've chosen images to cue data I can easily recall each day. Paul knew how to recall his position with Christ; he was seated at the table. David knew how to recall the protection of God; he was in a fortress, a tower, and a refuge, and he decorated this space in his mind with rocks, hands, the shadow of wings, and feathers to remember God's faithful and gentle care (Psalms 18:2, 35; 36:7; 91:4). Did David not understand—through memorable images of the fortresses and towers —His Savior? Did Moses not picture God as refuge and claim that "underneath are the everlasting arms" (Deuteronomy 33:27)? David, Paul, and Moses knew which images would most remind them of vital truths about God.

We have the same opportunity to consider biblical images to live in our identity in Christ each day. Like the biblical writers, we can inhabit the unseen place that God has built in our souls.

I want a life for you and for me that has learned to acclaim God and who walks all day long in the light of the presence of Jesus Christ. But first, we need to build a soul fortress to *remember.*

STIRRING OUR SOULS

—〰—

1. How do you best remember information?

2. Why do you think Christians don't always treasure God's Word? Read Psalm 119 in its entirety and note some of the benefits of reading God's Word.

3. What images come to mind when you think about God? Can you recall Bible verses that describe God with certain objects or everyday imagery?

4. What makes it so difficult to remember the truth about yourself and God each day?

—⟨⟨⟨—

CHAPTER 4

THE SOUL FORTRESS

The name of the Lord is a strong fortress;
the godly run to him and are safe.
—PROVERBS 18:10 (NLT)

He is my fortress, I will never be shaken.
—PSALM 62:2

I was a young mother when I read first read Psalm 90—an early psalm written by Moses. He writes such a strange little statement here. He says to God, "Lord, you have been our dwelling place."

I was deeply overcome by the thought that God was *my home* at that very moment. Perhaps it was because as a child from a military family, we had moved so many times; perhaps it was because we had bounced, in those first years of marriage, between apartment, church housing, and our first tiny house; perhaps it was because I lived such an unsettled, anxious life and wasn't sure where our ministry assignment would send us next—I just knew I was dwelling in God at that moment and nothing else mattered.

I could take Him, my True Home, wherever I was, and this reality shaped a new stability inside of me. In my inner being, I was always at home in God.

As time passed since I first noticed this verse—nearly fifteen years—I forgot how to inhabit this home, to really settle into this internal truth. One summer, I was working through a difficult realization regarding how destabilized I became in certain environments. The core of my being was rarely steady and differentiated from others around me. Social gatherings generated profound insecurity and self-evaluation. My counselor at the time had sent me an article on being a "self-differentiated adult." As I studied this concept, I found a helpful definition from psychiatrist Dr. Murray Bowen. He explains: "A person with a well-differentiated 'self' recognizes his realistic dependence on others, but he can stay calm and clear headed enough in the face of conflict, criticism, and rejection to distinguish thinking rooted in a careful assessment of the facts from thinking clouded by emotionality."[1]

Not only did I not feel like a real "self" inside, but I also had little emotional regulation, poor boundaries with people, and inability to "stay calm and clear headed" in any kind of distressing situation.

I wasn't strong inside. I was flimsy and empty. Even though I had realized I was seated with Christ in the heavenly realms, I was still learning how to internalize the biblical truths I read about God's presence in my soul, how to be strong and mature.

The Holy Spirit, who never stops working within us, used Psalm 90 to begin a process of strengthening my inner being that, over the course of the next few years, culminating in Psalm 97:10 and meeting my Guarding God, changed me. As I thought about "dwelling" in God—and how He was dwelling in me—I examined the idea of a fortress inside my soul. Many psalms point out being in a *fortress*. God was "my fortress . . . in whom I take refuge"; "Be my rock of refuge, to which I can always go . . . you are my rock and fortress" (Psalms 18:2; 71:3). Proverbs 14:26 tells us that "whoever fears the Lord has a secure fortress, and for their children it will be a refuge."

God is a *fortress*. The Hebrew words for these fortresses are beautiful and expansive. They evoke images of high towers stretching to the heavens, majestic castles, a defended high fort, and sturdy architecture. In other words: an impenetrable structure. Think of terraces and towers and beautiful palace doorways. Think of castles with spires and great halls and galleries. Think of the magnificent descriptions of ancient fortresses and palaces from David to Solomon to Herod relayed through biblical accounts, historians, and archeologists. Remember every movie you've seen with a fortress or castle in it.

The wonderful BBC series *Merlin* features the beautiful Château de Pierrefonds. There are also Neuschwanstein Castle, the nineteenth-century Romanesque Revival palace that provides the model for both Disney's *Sleeping Beauty's* and *Cinderella's* castles, and Pembroke Castle, the medieval castle featured in the BBC's *Prince Caspian*. If that weren't enough, we have Powderham Castle from *Robin Hood*, or, of course, Highclere Castle featured in *Downton Abbey*.[2]

Can you picture a fortress? Can you feel the cool stone against your hand and lift your eyes to the towering spires? Can you smell the expansive forest all around it and perhaps hear a jingling creek? What if such a place belonged to you and welcomed you inside its sturdy walls?

I wasn't familiar with thinking of my soul as dwelling in a fortress like this, but that's

WE NOW ABIDE "IN AN IMPREGNABLE FORTRESS INTO WHICH NO EVIL CAN ENTER AND NO ENEMY CAN PENETRATE."

what David did and I wanted to as well. David's fortresses could become as vivid a picture as Paul's seat in the heavenly realms. This was where I could live in my soul; yes, I could *live from my inner being* in these fortresses and castles and palaces and towers of stone. I loved that each castle or medieval fortress I pictured was indeed made from rock, as Scripture repeatedly calls God our rock and fortress. Here, I could dwell and finally find stability; the interiority of my life was not governed by my emotions, my interpersonal interactions, or my circumstances. The interiority of my life—my soul—was in a fortress.

God was my fortress. I chose this image just as the psalmist did as a structure to represent to their souls where God is dwelling and how. It is what Spurgeon calls our present "regal habitation."[3] Hannah Whitall Smith calls us to "surrender the central fortress of our nature to Him"[4] and says that we now abide "in an impregnable fortress into which no evil can enter and no enemy can penetrate."[5] Smith tells her readers that we move in to this fortress by faith and trust that we are, in fact, in the fortress of God in our inner being.

Day by day, I placed myself in the fortress. Yes, it was a castle I imagined with as much clarity as possible, much like the seat in the heavenly realms from Ephesians 2:6. Because the picture of my seat in the heavenly realms was based on Arthurian legend and the famed Knights of the Round Table, I picture King Arthur's castle in Camelot. Think of gothic architecture and all the trimmings: vaulted, arched ceilings, flying buttresses, ornate windows, and grandiose towers and spires. I even throw in some climbing ivy, stained glass, and clustered columns.

Imagining the fortress began to shape me into a different person; I was differentiated from people because I lived from my inner being. I could come and go from any situation, no matter how emotionally distressed, and stay in God's fortress. Here, I was safe, untouched, and unmoved.

I was in a fortress.

In rejection, I remembered I was in a fortress of God's care.

In any new, insecure environment, I was in a fortress of God's care.

When anxious due to any new circumstance, I was in a fortress of God's care.

When afraid, I was in a fortress of God's care and nothing could touch my soul.

That summer day when I read Psalm 97:10 and how God guards me, I thought of the fortress. But something was incomplete in my understanding. I wanted to know how God was guarding this fortress I had so carefully architected in my own soul. On my journey to maturity in the Lord, I began to flesh out the details of this fortress even more. I reasoned that I could build it and use visual cues, like Sherlock's brain attic, like the medieval Jews with their cakes and honey, and what I do as an educator to recall all the critical data needed about my soul each new day. It wasn't enough to vaguely imagine my soul in some kind of castle; I wanted to know what was happening inside that fortress. I did know at least one thing: I was seated at the greatest table with the greatest King in that fortress (Ephesians 2:6), but even more was happening than I could have ever imagined.

As I searched the Scriptures and I understood that Jesus was guarding me by His righteousness, peace, hope, power, and His crucified life, I enjoyed a season of fresh growth in my spiritual life. But I had to remember these truths. I had to do what the command in Revelation 3:3 outlines. Here God says, "Remember, therefore, what you have received and heard; hold it fast."

WE ARE GUARDED IN ALL OUR WAYS. WE ARE DWELLING IN HIM, AND NOTHING CAN TOUCH OUR SOULS IN THIS MOST MARVELOUS, SECRET PLACE.

I wanted to let these truths about my soul gain traction. I wanted to educate myself in how to retrieve data I needed from the Bible, in particular, about this fortress in my soul. In Psalm 71:3, David noted the importance of returning to the fortress of God's care. He writes, "Be my rock of refuge, to which I can *always* go; give the command to save me, for you are my rock and my fortress."

I think back to Moses and how he dwelled in so many distressing places but nevertheless knew a spiritual dwelling place with God. Many biblical scholars believe Moses wrote Psalm 91, and I read it with fresh eyes when I think about Moses wandering for years in temporary dwelling places. He that tells us in verses 1–2:

> Whoever dwells in the shelter of the Most High
> will rest in the shadow of the Almighty.
> I will say of the Lord, "He is my refuge and my fortress,
> my God, in whom I trust."

Moses imagined feathers and wings in this fortress when he writes, "He will cover you with his feathers, and under his wings you will find refuge; his faithfulness will be your shield and rampart" (v. 4). He didn't fear disease, suffering, or violence. He said instead, "If you . . . make the Most High your dwelling, no harm will overtake you, no disaster will come near your tent. For he will command his angels concerning you to guard you in all your ways" (vv. 9–11).

We are guarded in *all* our ways.

The primary reason why no harm or disaster overtakes our "tent" is because our "tent" is in the Lord. We are dwelling in Him, and nothing can touch our souls in this most marvelous, secret place.

Like Moses, let's seek to see this fortress in our minds—the strong, beautiful architecture—and may we know we are now living from this new, fortified inner being.

And now we might ask this question: What is Jesus doing in the secret place of our souls? And how can we internalize these truths to daily live in the reality of God's presence?

STIRRING OUR SOULS

—♒—

1. Which situations in your life (locations and people) most unsettle you, making you unable to stay calm and clearheaded?

2. When you imagine a fortress or a palace, what comes to mind? With as much detail as possible, describe or draw this structure.

3. Read Psalm 90 and make a note of your favorite verses. What difference does it make to you right now in your life to know that you are dwelling in God and He is dwelling in you?

4. What makes it so difficult for Christians to stay aware of God's presence inside them?

PART TWO

---ɯ---

IN THE SECRET
PLACE OF THE SOUL

———∿∿∿———

CHAPTER 5

THE CATAPULT: FROM CONDEMNED TO CONFIDENT

*What comes into our minds when we think
about God is the most important thing about us.*

—A. W. TOZER

*And the work of righteousness will be peace, and the
service of righteousness, quietness and confidence forever.*

—ISAIAH 32:17 (NASB)

G od's guarding presence in my soul as that beautiful fortress
needed some decoration. If I'm going to dwell there, as David
and Moses did, I wanted furniture to represent the aspects of God's
guarding care within me.

The first and arguably most important facet of His guarding
care is that we're protected by Christ's righteousness at all times.
We're clothed in it. We're completely covered by it. Because of this
declared righteousness, we move from condemned to confident
before God. Christ's righteousness applied to us makes us accept-
able to God at all times. We gain access to everything we need—
every spiritual blessing—from God because we've received

forgiveness of sins and can "approach [the] throne of grace with confidence" (Hebrews 4:16).

But what piece of furniture represents this confidence? Picture a catapult within the fortress. Maybe this seems like an odd object to choose, but you'll understand as I continue. For now, try to picture a catapult in your mind and keep reading.

As I look back on my journey as a Christian, I wonder why it took me so long to feel confident in my relationship with God. I battled feelings of condemnation for years. But when I remember that I'm guarded in the fortress of God's keeping care, I know that in this secret place of my soul, I'm guarded by righteousness. Scripture teaches that our faith in Jesus Christ secures right standing before God; Romans 3:22 states, "This righteousness is given through faith in Jesus Christ to all who believe." This means at all times, we confidently enter the presence of God.

I remember this confidence by the image of a catapult. I love this forceful, ballistic device that hurls me into the presence of God. I also picture a catapult because I wanted another "c" word to remind myself of truth each new morning.

I think of this old-fashioned ballistic device designed to hurl an object (the word *catapult* comes from the Greek word meaning to hurl): it's bulky, made of wood, with ropes and wheels and a giant bucket. Consider how, since the medieval period until today, the catapult is one of the most effective warfare mechanisms ever designed. Since I'm imagining my soul as an ancient fortress, I wanted to use the common weapon used to protect medieval castles. If you have trouble imagining a catapult, you can think of the many movies that feature them including *Chronicles of Narnia—Prince Caspian, Gladiator, Lord of the Rings, Night at the Museum, Robin Hood,* or *The Empire Strikes Back* to name a few.

So picture the catapult: We're not ever condemned before God. We're confident. We can catapult ourselves into His presence all day long, for whatever we need, and He's ready to receive us.

But maybe, like me, you don't believe you can act this way—this confidently and this boldly—with the God of the universe. You've been taught, perhaps, to live in guilt and unworthiness. Maybe you feel like a bother to God. Maybe you feel like He's too holy, and you must stay reverent, obedient, and in the corner.

But remember the catapult. And think of little children hurling themselves into a delighted Savior's arms, just like the account in the Gospels of the children coming to Jesus. They must have been rambunctious and annoying enough for the disciples to rebuke them, to keep them all away from the so-important Jesus. As the disciples try to shoo the jumping children away, I picture Jesus stooping down and gathering them all into His arms; I see all the children hurled as if from catapults into His lap. Jesus says in Matthew 19:14, "Let the little children come to me, and do not hinder them, for the kingdom of heaven belongs to such as these."

I can see myself hurling my whole body into God's great lap. Picture yourself along with me just flung into His presence. Picture those Internet videos of soldiers returning from deployment. Think of those children jumping all over that returning parent. Think of the love and the joy. Think of all that stored energy released as from a catapult. Children have such confidence before those they know love them absolutely and unconditionally.

Because Jesus says we must be "like a child" as we receive the kingdom of God (Mark 10:15), He covers me with His righteousness at all times, and I catapult myself into His arms each new day. I'm a child pummeling Him; I'm now lounging in His great arms. And God is absolutely delighted. He's thrilled I'm here. He's listening and ready to respond to whatever I need and He will do the same for you. Think of Zephaniah 3:17 (NIV 1984) and how God will "take great delight in you; he will quiet you with his love, he will rejoice over you with singing."

We move from condemnation to confidence; we can catapult ourselves right now into the presence of a God who's delighted and rejoicing over us and even singing about it.

Doesn't this sound so wonderful? I feel this way about Jesus now, but I didn't always. I wish I had learned sooner the truth of how God guards me with righteousness so I wouldn't have had to live in condemnation, hiding in the corner of God's throne room when I could have been catapulted right onto His great, loving lap anytime I wanted.

—◊◊◊—

There was a point in my life when, if you asked me what came into my mind when I thought about God, I would have used two words:

Distant.

Disappointed.

I believed God was distant because of all my sin. I understood the gospel—I was saved through God's gracious gift of salvation that I received through faith alone—but I still felt like my good behavior determined how God thought about me. I didn't have confidence about my relationship with God.

I grappled with the question of my guilt over sin and whether or not God was pleased with me. I've explained how a campus ministry staffer explained the simple truth: "There is now no condemnation for those who are in Christ Jesus." But I didn't always *feel* forgiven. I didn't always *feel* loved by God. I would read in Psalm 103:12, "as far as the east is from the west, so far has he removed our transgressions from us" and think that such statements could not possibly be true for me. Part of the problem was that I would experience such a satisfying walk with Jesus for months at a time,

MOST OF US HAVE TO LEARN THAT FAITH IS NOT A FEELING, AND THAT EVEN EXPERIENCING GOD'S FORGIVENESS DOES NOT DEPEND ON A FEELING; IT'S A *FACT*.

but then would fall back into old sin patterns. I didn't understand how to live a victorious Christian life. Instead, I often felt like a Christian failure and would then try harder to please God. It was a toxic mindset of trying to work my way out of condemnation.

Do you ever feel this way? Like you've ruined your life, like you've sinned too much, and that you're beyond forgiveness? Are you trying to please God by your good behavior now? Oh, how quickly we depart from gospel truth as soon as we're dealing with sin in our lives. How quickly we resort to winning God's affection through obedience and good works. What would it take to believe that we were declared, once and for all, righteousness before God? What would it take to believe that God sees us as holy and perfect because He sees Jesus when He looks at us?

And why do we base these truths on whether or not we have an emotional experience regarding them? Most of us have to learn that faith is not a feeling, and that even experiencing God's forgiveness does not depend on a feeling; it's a *fact*.

As I continued to steadily grow into the biblical mindset of being covered by Christ's righteousness, I would meditate on certain Bible verses to internalize the truth. In Isaiah 53:5 we read, "He was pierced for our transgressions, he was crushed for our iniquities; the punishment that brought us peace was on him, and by his wounds we are healed." I proclaimed this verse over my life and rejoice that Jesus was my healer even though I continued to feel accused and condemned. My mentor *told* me that the matter was settled; I was forgiven of my sin—past, present, and even future— and that God saw me now as pleasing to Him, fully accepted, and without sin because of Jesus. Even more, I had full access to this holy God because Jesus paid the penalty for my sin. Together we would read more of Romans 8 where Paul explains the reason why we don't live in condemnation or guilt. It's because "by sending his own Son in the likeness of sinful flesh and for sin, he condemned sin in the flesh, in order that the righteous requirement of the law might be fulfilled in us" (vv. 3–4 ESV).

Because of Jesus, we meet God's righteous requirement.

Because of Jesus, we're released from the punishment of sin.

Because of Jesus, we're not condemned.

No matter what.

This declaration is the most astonishing, history-changing, cataclysmic message to Satan: *You have no power to condemn me because of Jesus.* Jesus' death on the cross and His shed blood secured righteousness for those of us who have received Him. We're covered by it now and for always, and it extends into our past and far beyond ourselves to even atone for future sin. This good news provides an answer to the rejected, lonely, confused soul who now has been welcomed into God's presence and belongs forever in His family.

Now, even when we sin, we can simply confess our sin and restore our fellowship with Jesus based on the truth of 1 John 1:9: "If we confess our sins, he is faithful and just and will forgive us our sins and purify us from all unrighteousness."

This is true. This is true of my soul and yours right now. We in

Christ are not condemned. It doesn't matter what we feel about it; our feelings are not the truth.

The righteousness of Christ surrounds us, before and behind. Isaiah 58:8 tells us that "righteousness will go before you, and the glory of the Lord will be your rear guard." Righteousness is my *guard*.

This idea of being guarded by Christ's righteousness is the first piece of critical data I need to deposit into the fortress of my soul. We need this righteous guard because we have an accuser—Satan—who assaults us with condemnation day and night (Revelation 12:10). If you feel assaulted by feelings of worthlessness, shame, and guilt, it's no wonder: we have an enemy who doesn't want us to live in the reality of Christ's righteousness.

> OUR ACCESS TO A DELIGHTED, EAGER, AND LOVING GOD, BECAUSE OF JESUS' RIGHTEOUSNESS, IS THE BEST NEWS FOR ANYONE WHO FEELS SHE'S UNWORTHY AND A BOTHER TO GOD.

I knew it then and even more fully now: Within the fortress of God, I'm guarded at all times by Christ's righteousness. I saw myself as finally being "wrapped . . . with a robe of righteousness" (Isaiah 61:10 NASB) and protected by the "breastplate of righteousness" (Ephesians 6:14). In fact, the righteousness of Christ guards us on all sides. Guilt and shame should have no entry point. We are guarded by righteousness.

People guarded by Christ's righteousness move confidently into the presence of God. They move from condemned to confident. That alliteration reorients me each new morning. We know in Ephesians 3:12 that "in [Christ] and through faith in him we may approach God with freedom and confidence," so I became confident before God. Can you imagine it? Freedom and confidence to approach the Supreme Ruler of the universe? What a marvelous, nearly incomprehensible privilege!

We transform from condemned to confident. And we know God gives us what we need when we come into His presence. The writer of Hebrews insists we can "approach God's throne of grace with confidence, so that we may receive mercy and find grace to help us in our time of need" (Hebrews 4:16). I began to think not only that I had complete confidence to stand before God—not on my own merit but because of the sacrifice of Jesus Christ—but that God loved me and wanted me to come into His presence. In Isaiah 30:19, we are promised: "How gracious he will be when you cry for help! As soon as he hears, he will answer you."

Today in my neighborhood, I often tell my friends how I'm now using the image of the catapult to help me remember that because I'm guarded by righteousness, I can catapult myself into God's presence. I shared Bible verses about Jesus offering righteousness with a neighbor who was just beginning her spiritual journey with Jesus. She always felt like a bother, unimportant, and annoying to God. She felt unworthy. As we talked on the phone, she said, "Why would God listen to *me*? He's too busy! I'm a nobody and too unworthy." As a result of these feelings, she often sought out other sources—like Reiki healers, mediums, and psychics—to give her insight about her life. I told her that she could enter God's presence at any time because of Jesus. He made her worthy. She was important and very special to God. I also explained that she didn't need those other sources and that they were dangerous. She said abruptly, "Okay, goodbye."

"Wait a minute! Where are you going?" I cried, thinking I had offended her.

"I've got to go. I'm going to go talk to Jesus right now."

Our access to a delighted, eager, and loving God, because of Jesus' righteousness, is the best news for anyone who feels she's unworthy and a bother to God.

———❦———

As I meditated on both Romans 8 and Psalm 103 about not being condemned and God removing my sin, I realized the fact of my righteousness positions me before an attentive God. Soon my mind and emotions obeyed what I chose to believe was true of my soul.

I'm not *condemned*. I'm *confident*.

When we feel condemned, we can retrieve the critical data that we are guarded by Christ's righteousness and *silence the accuser of our souls*. We are *free to enter the throne room of God to make our requests and receive the help we need*. We have favor with a God who longs to be gracious to us and to bless us beyond measure.

We can have the scriptural truth and the corresponding mental picture to help bring the indwelling Christ to our minds. And all the while, we're fighting against the counterfeit, shadow narrative that runs alongside our souls, assaulting us with the world's and Satan's lies. Instead of confidence in Christ's finished work that declares our righteousness, the counterfeit is *working harder* to somehow earn God's favor.

In other words, we're tempted to *conform* or *correct our conduct* to be good, meeting all rules and standards in order to change God's opinion of us and put us in the position of blessing. This is not the gospel. People guarded by Christ don't conform or change their conduct first; they rather catapult their helpless, broken, dirty selves with confidence into God's presence, ask His forgiveness, and receive God's unlimited love, blessing, and favor because of Christ's righteousness applied to them.

—∞—

I'm dragging myself out of bed, and before my toes hit the worn carpet, I feel the weight of the day on my soul. I feel the creeping power of shame and guilt begin their encircling strangle. But I remember the words that parade in alliterative beauty across the landscape of my mind.

I'm confident before God and not *condemned.*

I'm catapulting into the presence of a God who is *captivated* by me.

I'm not *conforming* to rules. I'm *covered* by righteousness.

I recall the words and then Jesus. Immediately, He encloses my heart and soul in a guarding embrace. I've generated the soul fortress anew with the first piece of critical data: I'm not condemned. I'm confident. I'm catapulting myself into His arms. You can say this too.

And we can begin the day as a new person.

I'm a new creation, created to be like God in true righteousness (Colossians 3:10). I place myself under the guard of righteousness, and I know this essential truth:

Nothing can touch my soul today.

We're not condemned, not now and not ever. We confidently catapult ourselves into the arms of our Savior who loves us unconditionally, desires to bless us, and is working for our good.

STIRRING OUR SOULS

1. What comes to mind when asked the question "How does God feel about you?" Why?

2. Read Romans 8:1 and Psalm 103:12. What makes it so difficult to believe that God forgives, forgets, and no longer holds our sin against us?

3. How would your prayer life change if you knew you could "approach God's throne of grace with confidence"? (Hebrews 4:16)

4. What's the difference between Satan's accusations and knowing you need to confess sin to Jesus?

CHAPTER 6

THE MOAT: FROM HARASSED TO HARMONIZED

If you lose your reason, you lose it into the hand of God.
ELIZABETH GOUDGE IN *THE SCENT OF WATER*

Plenty of outward discomforts there may be,
and many earthly sorrows and trials
but through them all the soul that knows God
cannot but dwell inwardly in a fortress of perfect peace.
HANNAH WHITALL SMITH, *THE GOD OF ALL COMFORT*

During my late twenties, I became curious about what Christians meant by "peace."

I had settled the condemnation issue before God and lived with a new assurance of my salvation and confidence in my relationship with Jesus. But I went through many episodes when I was desperate for an inner experience of peace. The best way I can describe it was this profound sense that something was wrong. I felt an irrational dread that I tried to soothe with food, busyness, entertainment, exercise, and medication. Sometimes the stress felt like a black knot in my chest that would spread over my body until

I was shaking, sweating, and gasping for air. Every day felt like a struggle. Isaiah 57:20 described the sensation well: a "tossing sea, which cannot rest, whose waves cast up mire and mud."

Couldn't I just relax? Enjoy life? Just find some *peace*? So much in Scripture talked about peace, and I knew Jesus was called the Prince of Peace. I also knew the often-quoted words from Philippians 4:7 that the "peace of God . . . will guard your hearts and your minds in Christ Jesus." People quoted this passage all the time, but I couldn't figure out how to make it true for me. Can you relate? How would peace guard my heart? Oh, if only I could learn how!

Though I knew I was *confident and not condemned* before God, and I had the accompanying image of the *catapult* (so appropriate as I envisioned a towering medieval fortress), I now needed to understand God's guarding peace. What image could help me think about peace? What alliterative words could I find? And was this as important as I thought? Were Christians really guarded by peace? Was this an emotional experience or something else?

Surely I needed my soul guarded, rescued, kept by Christ's righteousness, but was peace as vital? I fiercely nodded my head in agreement when I read Hannah Whitall Smith's claim, "Of all the needs of the human heart none is greater than the need for peace; and none is more abundantly promised in the Gospel."[1]

This peace was promised; this peace could meet the greatest need of my heart.

I've been privileged to meet the traveling companion to Corrie ten Boom, the author of *The Hiding Place,* the engrossing account of how a Dutch Christian family helped many Jews escape the Nazi Holocaust. We follow Corrie ten Boom's imprisonment in horrific conditions and how she found strength, hope, and forgiveness in Jesus. A movie was made based on her book.[2]

Corrie's traveling companion and assistant, Ellen Stamps, was a visiting speaker at Camp Greystone, where I was working one summer. Mrs. Stamps shared many stories of her time with Corrie as they traveled the world together before Corrie died.

One day, Mrs. Stamps invited me to her guest cabin,

> "THE UPS AND DOWNS OF YOUR HEART ARE LIKE THE WAVES OF THE SEA, BUT THE HOLY SPIRIT IS A *CALM PLACE WITHIN YOU.*"

brewed hot coffee on a chilly, rainy day at camp, and prayed with me about my own life and struggles. I wrote in my journal everything I learned from this humble woman who had more wisdom stored in her than any person I had ever met. She talked to me privately—as the rain fell and the coffee brewed—to impart a few special lessons to me.

I felt so loved by God that He would allow me to spend time alone with such a godly woman. I wrote in my journal, "I think my life began to change on July 26," because Mrs. Stamps told me something very curious and new to me as I sat close beside her. I remember her soft hands. I remember how she held my hands in hers. I thought about all the hands she had held in her life of those who also needed to hear something about Jesus.

Mrs. Stamps looked at me and said this: "The ups and downs of your heart are like the waves of the sea, but the Holy Spirit is a *calm place within you.*"

I pictured in my mind some lake inside of me whose surface was smooth like glass. *The Holy Spirit is a calm place within me.* She conveyed many other lessons, but that statement struck me powerfully, and it was the one I remembered as I read Psalm 97:10 and learned about my Guarding God years later.

The Holy Spirit is a calm place within me. God is guarding me with His peace.

How do I get to this calm place within me where the Holy Spirit lives? When I think of God as the fortress within me, I add the image of that surrounding water—perhaps a moat to build up my medieval imagery—or some kind of lake reflecting the still forest all around. How wonderful to see that fortress inside of me and think about the classic form of water defense, the moat—present even in ancient times—within my soul. This water represented God's guarding peace surrounding my soul at all times. I loved this image of still, quiet waters, especially in light of Psalm 23:2–3 where David tells us that the Lord is a shepherd who "leads me beside quiet waters, he refreshes my soul."

But what trail led to that "calm place" inside? How would God lead me there? Nearly twenty years later, I found myself in a rocking chair reading *The God of All Comfort*, in which Hannah Whitall Smith describes a "fortress of peace" inside because of the indwelling Christ.[3] In my soul, I could access this mysterious thing called "peace." I became fascinated by this idea of peace that came, not through the mind or emotions, but from something else—the inner being that's being influenced, directed, and renewed by the Holy Spirit.

The biblical concept of peace is deeper and more beautiful than I had even imagined. The poet William Wordsworth describes experiences that "lie too deep for words" or "too deep for tears."[4] When I read about the Hebrew concept of *shalom* and discovered it means wholeness, tranquility, well-being, and harmony, I expanded my simple definition of peace to mean that "all is well" or "all is as it should be." But still, it seems too deep—too beautiful and powerful—for words. The Bible dictionary explained that peace was a "tranquil state of the soul assured of its salvation through Christ, and so fearing nothing from God and content with its earthly lot, of whatsoever sort that is."[5]

Can you imagine experiencing tranquility and being *content with your earthly lot, of whatever sort that is*? Can you imagine wholeness, well-being, and harmony? What would it look like?

I loved that word: *harmony*.

I thought about peace as *harmony*—with God, others, and myself.

I thought about peace as *alignment*—between my mind and Jesus'.

I thought about peace as *well-being*—where I feel "right" again because I'm accessing peace within my soul.

Paul's prayer in 2 Thessalonians doesn't hold back from a bold request. He writes in 3:16: "Now may the Lord of peace himself give you peace at all times and in every way."

At all times.

In every way.

Another version (NASB) puts it this way: "May the Lord of peace Himself *continually grant you peace in every circumstance.*" Can God continually grant me peace in every way? If I ask Him to, would He? And how would He do this? In Psalm 29:11, I read that "the Lord blesses his people with peace" and in Isaiah 26:3 that He "will keep in perfect peace those whose minds are steadfast, because they trust in [Him]." Would this perfect peace come via my emotions?

As someone who still endures bouts of anxiety, regular stress, and worry about my family's safety and health, I was beginning to

PEACE RULES US. PEACE BARRICADES US. PEACE GOVERNS US. JESUS, OUR PRINCE OF PEACE, GIVES US THIS DAILY PRIVILEGE OF COMING UNDER HIS RULING, GOVERNING, BARRICADING PEACE.

realize that, by faith, I could *choose* to believe my inner being was in perfect peace, despite what my anxious mind was doing. I could proclaim truth, dwell on the Scriptures, and picture the soul fortress of peace—and that protective moat—inside where Jesus is my Prince of Peace.

As I daily practiced a morning routine of *proclaiming the truth* that I was dwelling in Christ's peace, *meditating on the Scriptures*, and *picturing the fortress* and the smooth, calm water in my soul, my mind calmed down. It didn't always "work" to remove anxiety altogether, but remembering that I was guarded by peace was a foundation strengthened by physically and emotionally healthy choices. Essentially, my anxious mind no longer ruled me, determined truth, or dominated my behavior because I shifted my attention to my inner being where Jesus dwells. I believe my mind was finally aligning with what was true in my soul.

———⟋⟍———

We are blessed with peace. We are kept in peace. We do nothing but rest and receive. "Keep" in Isaiah 26:3 also means to "guard, keep, and blockade"—that extra form of guarding verb, *natsar*. It's the sense of how a watchman carefully blockades us on all sides with peace so nothing to the contrary can enter our souls. We are guarded, kept, and blessed with peace that works as a blockade against what unsettles us.

The image of ourselves being "blockaded" so nothing disturbs our peace offers us a fortifying image when anxiety threatens us. In Isaiah 60:17, God says, "I will make peace your governor and well-being your ruler." I wonder if this is a now-and-not-yet reality for believers at this moment. Can you imagine peace *governing you,* and well-being *ruling* you?

We don't have to be governed and ruled by anything other than peace.

The guarding image of peace continues in the New Testament when we read this very well-known passage of Scripture concerning peace. In Philippians 4:6–7 Paul writes:

> Do not be anxious about anything, but in every situation, by prayer and petition, with thanksgiving, present your requests to God. And the peace of God, which transcends all understanding, will guard your hearts and your minds in Christ Jesus.

The Greek sense of the word *guard* is to *come under the military protection of peace.* Again, we see the idea of the ruling power of peace when Paul writes in Colossians 3:15 to "let the peace of Christ rule in your hearts, since as members of one body you were called to peace."

Peace rules us. Peace barricades us. Peace governs us. Jesus, our Prince of Peace, gives us this daily privilege of coming under His ruling, governing, barricading peace.

We can simply, by faith, ask Jesus to let His peace rule in our souls. To remember how peace barricades us on all sides, protecting and guarding, picture the moat, crystal clear and still, around that fortress in your soul. Direct your mind, by the visual cue of the moat or still water, and then choose alliterative words as a memory prompt for the day. Think of this: If peace means harmony (with self, others, and God), you've moved from *harassed to harmonized and into the harbor of still waters.*

My method is to immediately move to an anchoring Scripture to connect me again to my Spirit-indwelt soul: I chose 2 Thessalonians 3:16: "Now may the Lord of peace himself give you peace at all times and in every way." You might find a different verse, perhaps something from Isaiah or Philippians. Whichever verse you choose, you have the memory aids you need: the harbor where you move from harassed to harmonized.

You have peace at all times and in every way. You can internalize this biblical truth.

Does this seem too good to be true? Does it seem inaccessible to you because you currently battle acute anxiety? Or are you in a particularly stressful season of life where nothing affords you peace? You might cry out, "Nothing works for me! I will always struggle!" What I've learned is this: dwelling from my inner being and choosing to believe that the Holy Spirit is offering His peace has, over time, soothed what I thought could never heal in me. It is not instant. I still struggle. But I trust Him more and more in this area and ask Him to help me experience the peace that is always available to me. And I've learned to ask the right questions about stress and anxiety. For example, I've learned to ask:

What is it that I'm really fearing and why?

Do I believe God keeps me and my loved ones in His guarding care, and that even death cannot separate us from this care?

I remember that it is well with my soul because even if my greatest fears come upon me, I am guarded, rescued, and kept by Jesus.

—∿—

Do you want the peace that Jesus offers? He says in John 14:27, "Peace I leave with you; my peace I give you. I do not give to you as the world gives. Do not let your hearts be troubled and do not be afraid." We can confidently ask for this peace because Jesus says He *gives it*. He *leaves it* for us. He gives it in such a way that we no longer have to be filled with trouble and fear. This is a kind of peace that the world cannot offer. We simply receive this peace by faith; it is the Father's will that we have this peace that Jesus freely gives, and if we ask anything according to His will, He hears us (1 John 5:14). Picture the smooth harbor in your soul fortress, and know you are there, dwelling in the peace that God offers.

The day hasn't even yet begun in full, and I'm guarded by peace. I head to the shower, first knowing I'm confident and not condemned; I've catapulted into His presence. Now, I know that I can move from harassed to harmonized; everything in my mind and in my life I ask, by faith, to align and live in agreement with Jesus. I pray this: "God, bring everything in my life into perfect harmony with You. If anything is out of alignment, and if I've let in any sources of harassment, please give me insight and power to recalibrate or remove that thing."

As I tell my mind to remember what's happening in my soul— I'm harmonized, not harassed—I feel, finally, like I'm accessing the "undisturbed places of rest" so promised in Psalm 23 and Isaiah 32. Isn't the whole Bible, after all, a story of leading people to their resting place? Just like the reality of being "seated with Christ" and the "kingdom of heaven is within you" are both now-and-not-yet realities, being guarded by peace is a present reality that will also manifest fully when we are resting in eternity with Jesus. But right now, we're here, resting in our soul fortress, guarded on all sides by peace.

But it's Wednesday, and so far, nothing is going according to plan. I'm having a terrible day: I have chills like I'm running a fever; I'm exhausted, moody, achy, and unmotivated for everything facing me. You know this kind of day. It's a day when the task of folding another load of laundry sends you into tears. You don't want to make dinner or clean up after anyone. You don't want to attend a meeting, give that presentation, or teach that class. You want to move out of your house and town and start a whole new, better life. Maybe you've received devastating news. Maybe you've been rejected, disappointed, humiliated, or harmed in some way.

So you cry. Maybe you even pound your fists on the table. You fling yourself on the unmade bed and say, "I hate everything. I can't do this anymore. I'm tired. I'm overwhelmed." So quickly do we leave the fortress of peace and undisturbed places of rest. This was my Wednesday, and I felt silly to have just written about peace when I couldn't now remember that soul fortress and that smooth, still water.

Sarah, our older daughter, slinks up beside me in the kitchen and places her hand on my shoulder. She's almost as tall as I am, so our eyes meet easily. "Mom," she says carefully and with authority, like I'm the child, "may I tell you something?"

She's so formal, so adult. She's the one who reminds me I'm seated with Christ when I feel jealous or compare my life to others. She continues, "You know how you're writing on how Jesus guards us?"

"Yes," I say, impatient and so worn out I feel it in my bones. My soul fortress seems more like a vapor—mist that's already dissolved by the heat of my bad mood—and I sink down against my daughter. I just can't find my way back to my soul's home with Christ. It feels so far away and inaccessible.

"Well, you forgot the most important way Jesus guards you."

"What? How?" I say, throwing my hands in the air like a bratty teenager in this role reversal in my own kitchen.

She pauses.

"He guards you from *yourself*."

She nods and raises her eyebrows in that knowing way that feels reprimanding but also so true that I actually gasp and can't find words.

Silence. I'm completely silenced by her. So she continues:

"Don't you think *I* have to ask Jesus every day to guard me from myself? How do you think I survive my own mind? I'm a mess inside! What would I do if Jesus didn't guard me from my own mind each day? Seriously, Mom! Ask Him to guard you from yourself, and He will!"

She floats off to finish her homework like she's in her own smooth moat around her soul fortress of peace.

I sneak away into a hot shower before I cook dinner, still silenced. I stand under the stream of water and hang my head in defeat. But it's the most victorious position I've been in all day. I can do nothing. I offer nothing, and I can't muster up the feelings of peace myself. I do nothing; Jesus does everything. *Jesus*, I say, *guard me from myself. Please. I just feel so messed up inside. I place myself under the ruling power of Your peace.*

Now the stones and bricks rise up around my soul into a glorious fortress—like Cinderella's magical gown that begins at her feet and swirls up into the most beautiful covering—as I begin to whisper the words: *Jesus, guard me from myself. I can't access Your peace, and I need protection from myself.* I think of Cinderella and how the most important part of her outfit wasn't the gown, it was her glass slippers, her *shoes*. I smile when I recall in Ephesians 6 that one of the pieces of armor we're to put on to stay "strong in the Lord and in his mighty power" (v. 10) is to have our feet "fitted with the readiness that comes from the gospel of peace" (v. 15). My glass slippers of the "gospel of peace" remind me that I'm walking into new, enemy territory as I battle to remember my own soul's position in Christ. So as Satan attempts to disturb this peace, I point to my shoes of peace. I'm covered, right down to my feet, by peace.

A weight fell off of me and went down the drain. I didn't have to manage my own peace or drum up some artificial sense of well-being. I could stand there like a small child with nothing to offer and just ask for what I need.

And He answered me. I began to believe that peace was guarding me, and whether or not I felt it in any emotional way, it was nevertheless true. As I told myself the truth—*I'm guarded by peace*—the bad mood lost its powerful sway. I went to make dinner in the calm lake of the Holy Spirit's peace. Living in that fortress of peace, I didn't have to be happy or mentally stable. I didn't have to be anything or do anything. I just had to go back to Jesus, my Savior, who rescues me, most of all, from *myself*.

I think about novelist Elizabeth's Goudge's character in *The Scent of Water* who fears she can never manage her own mind. A wise priest tells her, "If you lose your reason, you lose it into the hand of God."[6] When my own mind fails me and traps me in anxiety and disordered thinking, I know I'm kept in the hand of God. I'm kept in a fortress of perfect peace in my inner being. Knowing God holds even my mind in His hands comforts me in the face of aging with its accompanying possibility of dementia or memory loss, or a return of the anxiety and depression I once knew so well. My mind may fail me, but if I lose my mind, I lose it into the hand of God.

Remembering I'm guarded by peace challenges me more than anything else at this current stage of life. It's not simply that I've battled anxiety for so many years; it's that my culture packages so many counterfeits of the peace that Jesus offers.

There are any number of *false resting places* we may believe will bring the peace that passes understanding, and these things simply do not work. Rather than connecting with the Prince of Peace, they serve as counterfeit and diluted forms of well-being. These false resting places could be anything at all including health, emotional balance, wealth, marriage, thriving children, various New Age practices, or external environments like a perfectly clean home, vacation site, or new wardrobe. We need to remember that our soul finds rest in God alone, and that kind of peace nothing can destroy. This means that no matter where we are or what's happening to us, we can still dwell in that inward fortress of peace.

> WHAT A GRACIOUS, MERCIFUL GOD WE SERVE WHO DOES NOT ALLOW US TO FIND OUR REST AND PEACE APART FROM HIM!

As I was starting to know this truth in my soul, I thought of what my soul most needed all along. I thought of how Jesus had rescued us and could at all times provide us with peace. We are protected on all sides—guarded and kept—in this new dwelling place. God's righteousness—and now His peace—was building an unshakable fortress in my heart and mind.

I wanted what could not be shaken, and I was finally finding it. And I knew that all the pain of my life—all the sorrow, disappointment, loss, confusion, and wandering, had something to do with God delivering me from what could be shaken to what could never be.

Smith writes these key words: "When [the God of love] He sees His children resting their souls on things that can be shaken, [He] must necessarily remove those things from their lives in order that they may be driven to rest only on the things that cannot be shaken; and this process of removing is sometimes very hard."[7]

All the disappointments, rejections, and losses were the way I was indeed "driven to rest" in the Lord alone and no external thing. What a gracious, merciful God we serve who does not allow us to find our rest and peace apart from Him! Sometimes I wonder if God withheld a certain thing I wanted because I would have been tempted to base my peace and well-being on that thing—whether financial success, professional advancement, thriving children, or mental health. Instead, I've accumulated a lifetime of God's merciful refusals that drove me deeper into His lasting and wonderful peace.

If we are living in that place where God has shaken up our lives, allowed merciful refusals, or invited us into a season of suffering, we can approach Jesus with our need for Him and His peace and rest. We never have to work for this or manufacture it. We receive it. In Isaiah 63:14, the people "were given rest by the Spirit of the Lord." We might also apply Matthew 11:28 where Jesus says, "Come to me, all you who are weary and burdened, and I will give you rest." Finally, several times in the book of Hebrews, we're told to enter the rest of Jesus.

Sometimes the pathway to knowing this peace and rest comes about through suffering. Natural processes teach me this as I look at the lilacs in the backyard. I've been researching how to best preserve lilac bouquets in the house. I've learned that the lilac stem is so tough and thick that it's nearly impossible for those stems to draw up their life-sustaining nutrients in a vase. They wilt and expire within one day. I learn that you must *crush* and *split* the stems to soften them and provide many points of entry for the lilacs to suck up all the water.

I'm in the kitchen, damaging those stems—literally breaking them open with a knife (in order to save them!) and—I realize the tender hand of God in my own heart that crushes in order to provide a special and rapid access to what I really need: Him, the Living Water, my True Peace.

The tough, thick me softens so I can get what I've wanted and needed all along.

This suffering—in whatever form it's taking—is the crushing and cutting that saves us.

We enter into our soul fortress, resting our hand on that catapult and gazing at the smooth, clear water. We know that right now, we receive peace. We know that right now, we endure whatever pain God brings to remove any false resting place or counterfeit sources of peace. We also, because of God's love and tender mercy, invite any kind of crushing and splitting that brings us to the Prince of Peace. We surrender completely, and we rejoice that every bitter thing in our lives was a drawing toward our true Peace.

Andrew Murray writes, "All these searchings and hungerings and longings that are in your heart, I tell you they are the drawings of the divine magnet, Christ Jesus."[8]

That's what it was, always. All this life, a divine magnet.

We've been drawn to peace. We move from harassed to

harmonized. We're at rest, in perfect peace, and we recall the calm lake inside of our soul fortress. The day moves on: We are confident instead of condemned, catapulting ourselves into His presence. We're harmonized instead of harassed, and harboring on the smooth lake of our soul. It's a haven here, a place where vessels find shelter from rough waters. Return to the anchoring verse on peace from 2 Thessalonians 3:16: "Now may the Lord of peace himself give you peace at all times and in every way."

The waves crash out there, but in here, we're resting in the calm, perfect peace.

STIRRING OUR SOULS

1. What are (or what have been) some of your "false resting places" that you believe will bring you lasting peace?

2. How would your day be different if you were ruled and governed by peace? In what areas of your life are you not experiencing Jesus as the Prince of Peace?

3. Read Philippians 4:4–7. What do you think is the connection between rejoicing and thanksgiving and experiencing God's peace?

4. Explain what the quote "If you lose your reason, you lose it into the hands of God" means to you.

—⁓—

CHAPTER 7

THE WINDOW: FROM DESPAIR TO DELIGHT

Then swing your window open, the one with the fresh air and good eastern light, and watch for wings, edges, new beginnings.

—POET AND WRITER MONIQUE DUVAL

So far, we've learned how God dwells in our souls as a fortress, and in this refuge, we're guarded by His righteousness and peace.

Now let's explore another vital way God guards our souls:

We are guarded by *hope*.

Theologian R. C. Sproul wrote the following:

We were created for God. Just as fish are in despair out of water, so the human soul is in despair when it is outside of fellowship with God. . . . The goal of man is God. He is the fountain of peace, the wellspring of joy. We were created for happiness, not gloom. We were created for hope, not despair.[1]

We were created for *hope*.

We were created to know God, who is called in Romans 15:13 the *God of hope*, and like fish despairing out of water, we despair apart from dwelling with Christ in our souls. As we live in the fortress of God's guarding care, we can know Him not only as our righteousness and peace, but also as our hope. Paul writes, "May the God of hope fill you with all joy and peace as you trust in him, so that you may overflow with hope by the power of the Holy Spirit" (Romans 15:13).

If you look carefully, you'll note that we don't fill ourselves with hope; God fills us with joy and peace *so that* we will overflow with hope. He does this by the power of the Holy Spirit; we simply position ourselves to receive this overflowing hope. So many beautiful Greek words exist in this passage. We learn, for example, that whatever hope means, it's crammed in and "thoroughly permeating the soul"; that's the sense of fill in this passage.[2] We also learn that overflow means to have in abundance—so much so that it's leaking out. And finally, that beautiful biblical word, hope, means in the Greek, to "expect with pleasure good things." It means "to have a joyful and confident expectation of eternal salvation."[3]

We were created for this joyful, pleasurable hope. We dwell in hope as so wonderfully stated in Psalm 62:5 and proclaimed by Peter in Acts 2:26 that "my heart is glad and my tongue rejoices; my body also will rest in hope." We're also told in Romans 5:5 that "hope does not put us to shame, because God's love has been poured out into our hearts through the Holy Spirit, who has been given to us."

We dwell in hope.

We have a hope that does not disappoint us or put us to shame.

With hope, we have a confident belief and expectation of God's goodness to us, a confident belief and expectation that God is at work in the midst of any circumstance—with all His love and all His power working on our behalf—and a confident belief and expectation that Jesus guards our souls and provides everything we need at this very moment.

But remembering this hope, just like God's guarding righteousness and peace, can still be a challenge. John Piper warns that "hoping in God does not come naturally for sinners like us. We must preach it to ourselves, and preach diligently and forcefully, or we will give way to a downcast and disquieted spirit."[4] I indeed "give way to a downcast and disquieted spirit."

I too often dwell in despair instead of hope.

Piper encourages a diligent and forceful kind of preaching to ourselves each day. So I use the method of visual reminders, alliteration, and corresponding Bible verses as a diligent and forceful way to lead me back every morning to the God of hope.

I think about the dwelling place of God inside me: it's a soul fortress and refuge of righteousness, peace, and now hope, and I *choose* to receive the hope that the Holy Spirit pours out. I think of it as a window I can open when I'm in despair. It's a window that shows a new mercy of God despite circumstances. And I move from despair to delight because I dwell in hope.

Despair is the complete loss of hope. The Centers for Disease Control and Prevention reports that in 2015, 1.3 million adults attempted suicide and 9.3 million reported suicidal thoughts.[5] I know those thoughts. Many people are afraid to admit that they also know those thoughts. But they do. You are not alone if you are feeling despair. It's hard to talk about, so I understand why you don't share it.

Part of the reason so many people stay isolated in despair is that it's so difficult to describe. Some think of despair like this:

YOUR SOUL IS IN THERE, THE REAL AND TRUE YOU BURSTING WITH JOY AND HOPE, BUT YOU'VE LOST YOUR WAY TO HER. YOU FEEL LIKE A STRANGER TO YOURSELF. It's a haunting feeling that you're trapped and that something is irreversibly, permanently lost. It's a mired down, quicksand feeling that you're sinking into an abyss of regret and loss. It's a firm belief that nothing will change, that nothing will improve, and that you'll be in a prison of loneliness forever. It feels like you're living the wrong life, that someone has stolen your life, and that you've missed your chance at the life you were supposed to live. It's homesickness even when you're at home. It's a dark weight. It's an indescribable, suffocating, unseen pain. It's a kind of wrongness inside, an estrangement from yourself, and a colorless void. You tell people you're "tired" or "out of sorts." You tell people you "don't feel like going out today" or that you're "not yourself." You feel hopeless and confused. Your thoughts spin and spin. There's no beauty, no meaning, and no joy. Everything hurts, both inside and out. And the worst part is that you can't imagine any relief. The pain stretches out in a future that offers no relief and no comfort.

Your soul is in there, the real and true you bursting with joy and hope, but you've lost your way to her. You've lost your way home. It's a tangle, like a knot in your mind. You feel like a stranger to yourself.

At my worst in my late twenties, I would wake up with thoughts of death and imagine how easy and simple it would be to *just die*. So if you've felt these things, you are not alone. I went to many doctors and a skilled counselor who journeyed alongside me for several years to discover the source of my hopelessness. Was it medical, chemical, spiritual, relational? If I just exercised more, took medication, found some good friends, and prayed more, would I find hope again? Anyone who has been on the dark journey of depression knows that there's never an easy answer. It's never just one thing; it's always a combination of all of the above and often takes time to find mental health. While God used therapy, medication, nutrition, exercise, and recalibrating toxic or oppressive relationships to aid my own journey to heal from depression and anxiety, certain truths and biblical practices to usher in hope created the most rapid change and lasting transformation.

Your own journey is unique to you, but perhaps my journey into hope will spark something in you and transform that despairing feeling of dull, dark pain into delight. I have learned I can endure anything if I have hope. You can too. And hope has a name: Jesus is Hope. Our God is the "God of hope" (Romans 15:13).

But we also have an enemy, a "spirit of despair," at work against us. We can take great comfort in Isaiah 61—the same chapter Jesus quotes in the temple in Luke 4:18. In Isaiah 61:1–3 we read these words:

The Spirit of the Sovereign Lord is on me, because the Lord has anointed me to proclaim good news to the poor. He has sent me to bind up the brokenhearted, to proclaim freedom for the captives and release from darkness for the prisoners, to proclaim the year of the Lord's favor . . . to comfort all who mourn, and provide for those who grieve . . . to bestow on them a crown of beauty instead of ashes, the oil of joy instead of mourning, and a garment of praise instead of a spirit of despair.

Here, we see how Jesus is the one who bestows (gives freely, appoints, covers with) joy and praise. Jesus provides this covering—this surrounding, guarding joy and praise—instead of despair, and we can begin more and more to trust that our inner beings can access this joy and praise at all times. Jesus binds up our broken hearts, frees us from darkness, comforts us, provides for us, gives us beauty in places of ruin, and pours out joy. He calls it the oil of joy.

I married a man from North Carolina, and I love Southern cooking; I love to fry things in oil. If you've ever done this, you know the oil covers you, splattering everywhere and smelling up the whole house. Oil oozes out, flows freely, and wants to cover *everything*. I picture Jesus in the kitchen with me, pouring out the oil of joy all over the place.

As I position myself before God each day and imagine the fortress of righteousness, peace, and hope, three key questions help fortify my refuge in God where I dwell in hope. They are mindset shifters to move me from despair to delight and allow that oil of joy to flow.

Do I believe God is for me, not against me?
Will I forget the past and believe God is making a way?
Will I seek out the new mercies of God each new day?

QUESTION I:
DO I BELIEVE GOD IS FOR ME, NOT AGAINST ME?

My friend looked across the table at me where we were sitting at a restaurant. I was so depressed and hopeless that just leaving the house felt like a herculean task. Worse, I was angry, cynical, and mean. She softly asked, "Do you think God is against you?"

Oh, the question burned in my soul.

She quoted portions of Romans 8:28–37:

> We know that in all things God works for the good of those who love him, who have been called according to his purpose. . . . If God is for us, who can be against us? He who did not spare his own Son, but gave him up for us all—how will he not also, along with him, graciously give us all things?. . . Who shall separate us from the love of Christ? Shall trouble or hardship or persecution or famine or nakedness or danger or sword?. . . No, in all these things we are more than conquerors through him who loved us.

Part of my depression was that I fundamentally believed that *God was against me*. I fundamentally believed God was *withholding all things*. I felt *separated from His love*. I looked down into my lap and thought about her words and tears formed in my eyes. But they weren't tears of pain or sorrow or despair or longing.

They were tears of *hope* because the question invited the truth in.

Did I think God was against me? In other words, did I think He wanted me to suffer and live in misery? Did I not realize that God is for me? For me—as in truly working for my good at all times? Did I not realize that God will "graciously give all things"? Did I not realize that nothing could separate me from His love?

The question "Do you think God is against you?" reoriented me to the biblical truth that my soul dwells in the hope of this God who "works out everything in conformity to the purpose of his will" (Ephesians 1:11). The question, suddenly and powerfully, invited Jesus into my despair as an ally, not an enemy.

For the first time in months, I could say to Jesus: *We're together*

HOPE IS A VOICE OF RENEWAL, OF GROWTH, OF SPRINGING FORTH, AND OF IMPOSSIBLE ROUTES IN UNUSUAL PLACES.

in this. I'm not alone, and You are not against me. You are for me, working for my good all the time. Nothing, not even this despair, can separate me from Your love, Jesus.

As I trusted that God was "for me," I could then surrender to His plans for my life—to live the life He wanted me to live—and to relax into His care. No matter what my circumstances looked like or how my brain suffered, I knew that God was with me and nothing could separate me from His love. When I acknowledged that Jesus was here, with me and for me, a crack opened up in my angry, sullen, cynical, and hurting soul, and light flooded in through that window of hope.

Believing that God was for me, not against me, provided the foundation for any kind of lasting change in my soul.

—∞—

QUESTION 2:
WILL I FORGET THE PAST AND BELIEVE GOD IS MAKING A WAY?

I was riding on a train from Virginia to Connecticut for a work commitment when I came across Isaiah 43:18–19. God says here, "Forget the former things; do not dwell on the past. See, I am doing a new thing! Now it springs up; do you not perceive it? I am making a way in the wilderness and streams in the wasteland."

At that moment, I realized how much I was dwelling in the past. Instead of dwelling in hope, I was too often still dwelling in shame, regret, and longing. On that train with my Bible, I pondered: *Will I stop living in the past and consider that God can make a roadway in the wilderness and streams in the desert? If I don't dwell in the past, where will I dwell?*

I knew it then: I needed to learn to dwell in hope. God was doing something; did I not perceive it? No, I did not, but I would learn to.

Hope is a voice of renewal, of growth, of springing forth, and of impossible routes in unusual places. Could I believe that God would "make a roadway" in what I perceived as the wilderness and desert of my heart? I turned next to Isaiah 40:2, and I underlined these words: "Speak tenderly to Jerusalem and proclaim to her that her hard service has been completed, that her sin has been paid for." One version says, "Tell her that her sad days are gone and her sins are pardoned" (NLT).

Her sad days are gone. Could I believe it? Can you? Hope burst in through the question, "Will I forget the past and believe that God is making a way for me?"

People guarded by hope live in the reality that God is *always making a way.* They do not live in the past. They can be like Joseph, who, in Genesis 41:52, names his second-born son. In this simple phrase, no more than a few words, God revealed to me a principle that let the tiniest ray of light into my heart. A window opened, and I moved from despair to delight. The author writes this stunning statement: "The second son he named Ephraim and said, 'It is because God has made me fruitful in the land of my suffering.'"

I repeated the phrase over and over again for days. *God has made me fruitful in the land of my suffering. God has blessed me in the place of my suffering.*

Our God of hope makes a way and blesses us in the very place where we feel we suffer most. If I could believe this, I could dwell in hope for the rest of my life.

—⟶⟶—

QUESTION 3:
WILL I SEEK OUT THE
NEW MERCIES OF GOD EACH NEW DAY?

So far, I believe that God is for me, and I choose to believe He is making a way in what I perceive to be the wasteland of my life. But the third question to fortify hope is this:

Will I seek out the new mercies of God each new day?

The prophet Jeremiah describes the hopeless soul best in Lamentations 3. This chapter describes a man who claims he dwells in darkness, feels walled in, mangled, deprived of peace, and who experiences that God's hand is against him. He's afflicted, tormented, and despairing. Jeremiah further writes in verses 18–24 some of the saddest yet ultimately hopeful words in the Bible:

> I say, "My splendor is gone and all that I had hoped from the Lord." I remember my affliction and my wandering, the bitterness and the gall. I well remember them, and my soul is downcast within me. Yet this I call to mind and therefore I have hope: Because of the Lord's great love we are not consumed, for his compassions never fail. They are new every morning; great is your faithfulness. I say to myself, "The Lord is my portion; therefore I will wait for him."

The despairing impression, "all I had hoped from the Lord is gone," can't possibly be worse. Yet Jeremiah chooses to call something to mind that brings hope: He looks for the new work of the Lord each new day. He admits to his soul that God's compassions never fail. They are "new every morning." I imagine what it takes for Jeremiah, in the midst of such pain and internal trauma, to think of the new mercies—or compassions—of God every new morning. He moves from a toxic, despairing mindset to a biblical mindset of hope.

Choosing to look for the "new mercies" of God each morning for me became a spiritual practice to build hope. I had to fight the despair. I had to find a way to stay afloat in hope when drowning in depression. It was that diligent and forceful daily preaching of hope to my soul. This practice corresponded with my desire to write again, and my friend Laurie first suggested my daily recording of new mercies in a blog format for others to read. We were having coffee together, and Laurie said, "You're a writer; you should write." But it felt hopeless to write. I had endured a decade of rejection letters from publishers. "You should blog. I would read your blog," Laurie said.

Hope rose up in my heart that stored so many words just waiting to get out. I remembered the day I stood crying before a wall of letters displayed at Carl Sandburg's home in Flat Rock, North Carolina. One was a postcard that Sandburg's wife wrote to him when he had lost hope about his writing. She wrote: "The Poems are great, Carl. . . You've got it in you. The only question is can we get . . . it out of you! You are great and great and great!"[6] Maybe the writing was in me; I just had to get it out. It's the same statement I say to my students each semester: "I know the writing's in you. We just have to get it out of you. You are great and great and great!"

And so I started writing each day and didn't stop for thousands of days. I followed hope every single day. Battling depression, anxiety, and days upon days of unstable emotions, I nevertheless chose to wake up and trust that God had some beautiful moment for me to observe and record. My blog at the time, *Live with Flair*, was a catalogue of new mercies to help me call to mind and have hope that the Lord was here and working. Each day, I found some little inkling—some moment of curiosity or wonder—to showcase God at work in some way. I blogged every single day—sometimes just a few sentences—to record *something good*.

I do this, and continue to do this, because this practice has changed my brain. I learned a mindset of "living with flair," which meant that my readers and I would find some moment to marvel over, no matter how sick, bored, disappointed, angry, or anxious I was. Every day became a hunt, a mystery, a wonder. The more boring, the more challenging. The more sad I felt, the more hopeful I was that the flair moment would be that much more meaningful and vibrant to me. I believed God was at work, and I would find it no matter what. I "found the flair" in everything from acorns to compost, from dentist appointments to spilled grape juice. I considered soap, coats, the whorls of tree trunks, scars, candles, milk, and kites. Every single thing I observed became fertile soil for planting hope.

Blogging every day *for thousands of days* helped build hope where there was no hope. I had to trust and depend on the Holy Spirit every single day *to show me something good*. I would roll out of bed and say, "Okay, God. I post the blog by 7:00 p.m., so we have exactly twelve hours. Would You show me something good? Help me find it. Help me see You, Jesus." I thought of Psalm 4:6–7 (ESV) when David questions along with many others, "Who will show us some good?" The Lord can. Jesus shows us good things each new day to fill our heart with joy. David continues, "'Lift up the light of your face upon us, O Lord!' You have put more joy in my heart than they have when their grain and wine abound."

As I wrote each day, I noted that the joy was already there; I just had to recognize it again. I could learn to identify joy. I could learn to identify hope. I could *train my mind* in joy and hope. I was living with flair, and my God of Hope won the day. This was a miraculous soul transformation rooted in the spiritual practice of seeking God's daily new mercies.

I woke up to hope instead of despair, to gratitude instead of anger, to worship instead of cynicism. I woke up with energy and joy. I woke up eager and deeply connected to people who read my blog and wanted to talk about it. And when a hard morning came through illness, rejection, or loss, I could open a window and choose to see God's wonder and blessing in some hidden place. Literally, I learned to open a window: I blogged for years about the weeping cherry tree outside the bedroom window through every season.

I found beauty in ice, in stark emptiness, in vibrant blooms, and in robins' eggs and hummingbirds. Outside the kitchen window were northern cardinals, the growth of the blackberries, sunsets, and lilacs. I opened the window and followed hope. I learned spiritual principles from snowflakes, berries, weeds, and acorns. I learned about my own soul as I watched the seasons go by for years from that window's view.

What are you learning about your own soul? How are you learning to "live with flair," to find new mercies to marvel over? And perhaps might you showcase what you're learning in a creative way, like writing or painting or other outlet? Maybe, like Carl Sandburg's wife said, is there something in you that needs to get out through a form of expression?

In our soul fortress, where we're guarded by hope, we open the window. No matter what's happening around us, there's always a window to look out and perceive the beauty, goodness, and power of God at work. We need the Holy Spirit to give us new eyes to understand hope. I pray for you what Paul prays in Ephesians 1:18 that *the eyes of your heart may be enlightened in order that you may know the hope to which He has called you.*

Ellen Stamps, the woman who said that the Holy Spirit was a calm place within, taught me, simply and directly, something about the voice of God. She said, "The Holy Spirit is always a voice of hope. Don't listen to any voice that isn't hope." My heart only knew how to listen to despair. I thought nothing would ever change. I thought God could never heal someone like me who had strayed too far. I thought God had no future for me. Sadness was my skin.

But in our soul fortress, we open the window. We remember *hope.* We turn despair into delight because of the operative power of hope. Because the Holy Spirit is a Spirit of hope, we know that we're indwelt with this hope. Some mornings, the old despair returns, and I have to *choose* hope. I cannot listen to discouragement or fear. And I'm trying to teach my daughters how to wear hope like skin, to let it guard everything about them. I'm trying to tell them that they must always listen to His voice of hope and no other voice.

My daughter reports with joy her Sunday school lesson on John 15 and how, if she stays close to Jesus, her life will bear fruit. She sounds so hopeful as she explains the gardening metaphor. "If I'm an apple seed, I will bear *apples.* I don't need to be an orange or wish I were a banana tree if I'm an *apple.*"

I think about self-acceptance and surrender. I think about how God ordains the life we have and how it took me forty years to articulate this very thought. She is talking about comparing her life to others, especially in school and when she sees other girls excelling in so many ways.

"WHEN I AM HAVING DARK DAYS, I REMEMBER THAT SOME PLANTS NEED SHADE TO GROW BEST. MY LIFE MAY NEED MORE SHADE THAN OTHERS, AND THIS IS HOW I'LL GROW."

I see hope in her for the first time in days. Then later, as we're walking the neighbor's old dog (the one we have to walk slowly because she's so very old), she says, "And do you know what? I shouldn't worry if other girls seem so happy and have wonderful things happen to them. It's like they have sunshine in their lives every day. I get jealous of all that sunshine. I have dark days."

I nod in silence as we walk the old dog slowly.

She prattles on, but I'm stuck on her statement about the dark days. That's me. That's us. We have dark days.

"And then I thought of the gardener and vine," she says, bouncing ahead and then circling back to the slow dog. "When I am having dark days, I remember that some plants need shade to grow best. My life may need more shade than others, and this is how I'll grow."

Some plants grow best in shade.

I think about my dark days and all the ways God grew me from that soil. It was the darkness I needed to germinate and grow.

She tells me I can share her hope with others. *If it's a sad day, remember that some plants grow best in shade.*

We both are finding hope in the shade.

—∽∽—

As I rest in this overflowing hope Jesus gives, I remember what might serve as a counterfeit to biblical hope. The counterfeit to righteousness is a "work harder, obey more" kind of mentality, and the counterfeit to peace is any kind of activity that promises well-being apart from Jesus. So the counterfeit to biblical hope is a prosperity gospel mindset that insists our hope is in material possessions, better health, or greater success. That kind of hope guards us by our circumstances rather than the confident expectation of God's salvation and presence in our life.

Our hope isn't in our possessions, our health, or our success. Our hope isn't even in our nation, our leaders, or our laws. Chuck Colson, the founder of Prison Fellowship, claimed in a speech made famous by its inclusion in the prologue to Steven Curtis Chapman's song "Heaven in the Real World" the following:

> Where is the hope? I meet millions of people that tell me that they feel demoralized by the decay around us. Where is the hope? The hope that each of us has is not in who governs us, or what laws are passed, or what great things we do as a nation. Our hope is in the power of God working through the hearts of people. That's where our hope lies in this country. And that's where our hope lies in our life.[7]

Colson's words offer a mindset as I think about, not just my own life, but our nation. When I feel scared or troubled or feel the old despair creeping back, I remember that my hope is in "the power of God working" and not in our nation or its leaders.

Just as how I once sought so many "false rests" to afford my soul peace, many of us often move to the counterfeit sources of hope including wealth, health, and systems of government. Our hope must rest in one thing alone: Jesus Christ, the God of hope, who fills us to overflowing with this hope we need more than air. Outwardly, we can waste away, but inwardly, we're renewed in hope.

Know that God is not against you and that nothing separates you from His love.

Know that you can forget the past and believe God is making a way forward for you.

Know that you can find new mercies each new morning of your life.

May we all be guarded by hope, and remember it with the window and the despair that turns to delight. And may the window lead us back to Romans 15:13: "May the God of hope fill you with all joy and peace as you trust in him, so that you may overflow with hope by the power of the Holy Spirit."

As someone who wakes up to hope now, instead of despair, I move through the images:

A catapult: I'm confidently moving into God's presence because I'm not condemned. I quote Romans 8:1.

A calm lake: I'm harmonized instead of harassed. The Holy Spirit is the harbor within me, and I can dwell there. I quote 2 Thessalonians 3:16.

And now? Instead of despair, I live in *delight*. The image I use to remember is a window that opens to let the light and new, fresh air into my soul. I ask God to remove the spirit of despair and replace it with the spirit of hope. No matter how dark the circumstances, there's always a window to open to perceive the beauty of God and to rest in His hope that He has power "that enables him to bring everything under his control" (Philippians 3:21). I fling open the window in my soul and proclaim that nothing can separate me from His love. I proclaim that right here, right now, God is not against me but for me. I set up the military guard of hope around the boundaries of my soul. I cry out, like David, "Show me the wonder of Your great love!" and then I wait, observe, and record the beauty in this ordinary day.

And I do it again each new morning.

Consider the inspiring words of Monique Duval, who said, "Then swing your window open, the one with the fresh air and good eastern light, and watch for wings, edges, new beginnings," or the great poet Elizabeth Barrett Browning, who said that she "opened wide the window of her soul."

I swing wide open the window of my soul and take in all the hope Christ offers.

STIRRING OUR SOULS

—⟨⟨⟨—

1. Do you believe God is for you and not against you?
   Read Romans 8 and write your own response to God
   about His love for you.

2. How are you still dwelling in the past? What would it
   take for you to forget the past and believe God is making a way?

3. Begin the practice of seeking out God's new mercies.
   Write down at least three things you want to recognize
   about God's work in your life on this day. Or even consider doing this every day for at least a month.

4. In what ways might you creatively express what you are
   learning about God's new mercies?

—∿∿—

CHAPTER 8

THE ARM: FROM FRAGILE TO A MIGHTY FORCE

The Lord will fight for you; you need only to be still.
—EXODUS 14:14

In addition to the teaching of God's Word, the Holy Spirit in His gracious work in the soul declares His own presence. Through His agency we are "born again," and through His dwelling we possess superhuman power.
—D. L. MOODY IN *SECRET POWER*[1]

I remember exactly where I stood when I heard a woman say something so astonishing it produced a tectonic shift strong enough to create an earthquake in my soul.

I was in the living room of the home I rented as a graduate student, and my friend said casually, "I can't believe I once tried to live the Christian life in my own strength. I had never heard of the Spirit-filled life before, but knowing now that Jesus gives me power to live a supernatural life has made all the difference."

I nodded my head slowly and smiled like someone listening to a stranger speaking in a foreign language when I didn't want to admit I had no idea what she's saying. What did she mean she wasn't living her life in her own strength? And what did she mean by power?

A short handbook called *Practical Christian Living* explains how we access the unlimited power of God. Simply put, if we express our desire to be controlled by God's Spirit, confess any known sin to Jesus, and then, simply by faith, appropriate God's power in our lives, that power is now fully operative.[2] Jesus claims, "You will receive power when the Holy Spirit comes on you" (Acts 1:8), and instructs the disciples to wait until they "have been clothed with power from on high" (Luke 24:49). Even more, read in John 3:34 where Jesus says that God "gives the spirit without limit."

WHATEVER THIS POWER IS LIKE, WE KNOW THAT IT'S THE SAME KIND OF POWER THAT RAISED CHRIST FROM THE DEAD.

The Holy Spirit was power. We receive power; Jesus clothes us with power; He gives it without limit. We have the Holy Spirit *without limit*.

I wanted to feel powerful, but I felt fragile and weak instead. I didn't feel like anything about my life was "supernatural," or that I had the "superhuman power" that the great revival preacher D. L. Moody insisted Christians possess. Do you? Wouldn't it be incredible if we did? Can you imagine a life lived in superhuman power?

Scripture teaches that a God with unlimited power guards us, and this power is available to us through the Holy Spirit. I can hardly understand it; it takes my breath away. I was learning that He was *in* even *me*, living even in my soul, activating me somehow, and giving me power in every situation. I feel silly and immature when I think about the power that's readily available that I ignore and waste each day. I'm sulking around my house, bored and moody, when infinite power resides in my soul.

In light of such truth, I snicker at the weary voice that says, "I can't do this."

Of course I can't do this—whatever *this* is—but "I can do all this through [Christ] who gives me strength" (Philippians 4:13). Just as I needed a way to inhabit Christ's righteousness, peace, and hope, I now needed to understand the power a Christian possesses. In Ephesians 1:17–20, Paul writes:

> I keep asking that the God of our Lord Jesus Christ, the glorious Father, may give you the Spirit of wisdom and revelation, so that you may know him better. I pray that the eyes of your heart may be enlightened in order that you may know . . . his incomparably great power for us who believe. That power is the same as the mighty strength he exerted when he raised Christ from the dead and seated him at his right hand in the heavenly realms.

Paul prays that we have a Spirit of wisdom and revelation to know this power. Whatever this power is like, it's the same kind of power that raised Christ from the dead. In other words: supernatural, miraculous, and so beyond human understanding that we need a Spirit of wisdom and revelation to know it.

If you notice from the above passage, we do nothing to earn this power. Paul doesn't say we must work harder, sacrifice anything, attend any meeting, or pay dues for it. He doesn't even say we must pray more, serve more, worship better, or anything else. He just urges that we would *know what is true about us right now and what is available to us right how.*

This is so wonderfully strange, so nearly absurd to the scholarly mind, yet so very true. What other religious system promises that a miraculously resurrected, living God takes residence in the human soul and gives power to do impossible things? What other religious system invites its followers to exchange their very being—to metaphorically crucify it by an act of their will—to receive another Life that inhabits them?

Paul writes in Galatians 2:20, "I have been crucified with Christ and I no longer live, but Christ lives in me. The life I now live in the body, I live by faith in the Son of God, who loved me and gave himself for me." This gospel isn't only about receiving forgiveness of sins; it's about what happens at the point of that forgiveness and how salvation includes a profound soul transaction. We become people possessed by a living Christ of infinite power. One preacher says it's a different life of "impossibilities made possible and actual by God's almighty power."[3]

—◌◌◌—

How would I live this day differently with this power that "works impossibilities" all day long? How would this ordinary day now burst at the seams with supernatural power?

Consider, first of all, what we need so much power for. I discovered most importantly that the power that raised Christ from the dead also raises to life our own dead and enslaved spirit, and now this power infuses our whole being. This is a guarding power that transfers us from the power of Satan into the loving domain of our Savior.

Scripture teaches that we are "under the power of sin" and held by "the power of Satan" (Romans 3:9; Acts 26:18). When we receive Christ into our lives, we come under the guarding power of

Jesus. First Peter 1:5 insists that we are "shielded by God's power"; Jesus' death and resurrection broke the power of sin and the power of Satan in our lives. In fact, the Greek verb "to break" that describes how Jesus breaks the guarding

THROUGHOUT SCRIPTURE, WE SEE THE PICTURE OF GOD'S MIGHTY ARM.

power of sin in our lives is one that means "to render inoperable, ineffective, unemployed, idle, deprived of force, and completely severed."[4] Sin and Satan stay inoperable, ineffective, without force, and removed from us as we remain guarded by God's power.

Thinking of God's power as a shield was one way I could picture this concept, but what helped me remember even more was the same image of power that Moses, David, and Isaiah called to mind. We even have words from the Lord Himself using this image. In Psalm 89:21, God says, "My hand will sustain him; surely my arm will strengthen him." Throughout Scripture, we see the picture of that mighty arm and the hand. For example, in Isaiah 59:1, we read that "the arm of the Lord is not too short to save" and how God has a "mighty hand and an outstretched arm" (Deuteronomy 4:34). The prophet Isaiah, after all, said to the Lord, "Be our arm every morning" (Isaiah 33:2 ESV).

That word, *arm*, was Isaiah's symbol of the Lord's strength, and I choose it as mine as well. Yes, I picture a great, hairy arm—all bulging muscles and popping veins—right there in my soul fortress.

As I move into the day, I recall the catapult of confidence, the calm lake of peace, and the window of hope. I bring my soul fortress into focus. I praise Jesus because here with Him, I move from condemned to confident, from harassed to harmonized, from despair to delight. And now, I recall the arm of the Lord and His power.

—⟨⟨⟨—

You might wonder how this power works most in our ordinary days, and perhaps you have images of yourself performing miracles at your desk or as you're cleaning the kitchen. But really, one of the most significant demonstrations of the Spirit's power in our lives isn't healing or miraculous provision but the miracle of how God molds our character to be like Jesus.

Someone has said that the definition of spiritual maturity is responding with Christ's character in all situations. Think about the power it would take to radiate Christ's presence and character in every circumstance of your life. By God's power—and not from our own strength or self-effort—we can grow into this kind of maturity.

It's just 7:30 a.m., and I've already failed. I've snapped at my daughter who just wanted me to braid her hair, and I've grumbled instead of rejoiced over the day of campus work ahead. I want to stay in my pajamas and give up on this day. I know I can move forward and say, "Jesus help me live this day," and I also confess my self-effort and sin of relying on any other source of strength.

The prophet Jeremiah understood the importance of relying on God's strength alone, especially as he records a dire warning from God about this very issue. He writes: "This is what the Lord says: 'Cursed is the one who trusts in man, who draws strength from mere flesh and whose heart turns away from the Lord'" (Jeremiah 17:5). Indeed, perhaps our greatest sin isn't these outward things we so easily condemn ourselves for, but something deeper and more insidious. Perhaps the greatest sin is any attempt to draw strength from a source other than the Lord.

The New Testament writers took seriously the idea of trusting and relying exclusively on God's power. Paul states succinctly that

"I can do all this through him who gives me strength" in Philippians 4:13, and in 1 Peter 4:11, we're told to serve with the "strength God provides" so that God received the praise through Jesus Christ. We're told to "be strong in the Lord and in his mighty power" and that this power accomplishes "immeasurably more than all we ask or imagine" (Ephesians 6:10; 3:20).

Paul also provides insight into what we need so much power for. He writes in Ephesians 3:16–19:

> I pray that out of his glorious riches he may strengthen you with power through his Spirit in your inner being, so that Christ may dwell in your hearts through faith. And I pray that you, being rooted and established in love, may have power, together with all the Lord's holy people, to grasp how wide and long and high and deep is the love of Christ, and to know this love that surpasses knowledge—that you may be filled to the measure of all the fullness of God.

Paul writes that we need this power in our inner being so Christ may *dwell* in us, so we *experience* His love, so we are *filled* to the fullness of God, and that God's power, as shown in verses 20–21, *operates* in us to do things. We need Christ's power to know the Christ we possess in our inner beings.

It's settled: I require power today in my inner being that will allow my mind to lay hold of God's love and energy within me. I want this power that allows God to do "immeasurably more than all we ask or imagine." We need to remember that God takes every detail of our lives under this guarding power. We read clearly in Philippians 3:21 about this power "that enables [Jesus] to bring everything under his control," yet how easy it is to forget this power that's here within us right now.

But it's not only us. The whole nation of Israel forgot God's power and the prophet Isaiah had to remind them with these famous words:

> Why do you complain, Jacob? Why do you say, Israel, "My way is hidden from the Lord; my cause is disregarded by my God"? Do you not know? Have you not heard? The Lord is the everlasting God, the Creator of the ends of the earth. He will not grow tired or weary, and his understanding no one can fathom. He gives strength to the weary and increases the power of the weak. Even youths grow tired and weary, and young men stumble and fall; but those who hope in the Lord will renew their strength. They will soar on wings like eagles; they will run and not grow weary, they will walk and not be faint. (Isaiah 40:27–31)

It's fascinating that Isaiah taught the people to remember the power available to them through the memorable visual cue of the eagle. Israel complained because they felt ignored and weary and weak. So Isaiah reminds them, with a relevant image, what it's actually like to know God's power. *Think of an eagle; this will remind you.*

Imagine the complainers Isaiah was addressing as they looked up into the sky to watch the soaring eagles. Eagles spend less than two minutes per hour flapping their wings. For almost 96 percent of the hour, they're relaxing. These magnificent birds flap for a little bit and then they know how to use something unseen but nevertheless operative: the thermal air columns beneath them. In other words, the flapping takes a great deal of energy, so eagles soar from another power source. They use little energy of their own because they depend on the thermals.[5]

I lean back in my chair: I want to depend on Holy Spirit thermals.

Eagles know this power available to them, so they cease striving. They know that an energy source exists that they can tap into. So they rest and soar. The eagle doesn't consider how impossible, counterintuitive, or imaginative this whole soaring business is; after all, nobody can see the thermals, just as nobody can see the Holy Spirit.

Nevertheless, the eagle just soars. He just throws himself upon the unseen air current. I think of those strong wings that could try to fly on their own strength. I think of how an eagle seems so powerful and intimidating. But he relinquishes that power and surrenders to another source.

He rests and soars.

Think of the eagle, and think of our lives resting and soaring by God's power within. Major Ian Thomas, in *The Saving Life of Christ*, explained this rest well when he wrote:

> If you will but trust Christ, not only for the death He died in order to redeem you, but also for the life that He lives and waits to live through you, the very next step you take will be a step taken in the very energy and power of God Himself. You will have begun to live a life which is essentially supernatural, yet still clothed with the common humanity of your physical body. . . . You will have become *totally dependent* upon the life of Christ within you, and never before will you have been so *independent*, so *emancipated* from the pressure of your circumstances, so released at last.[6]

I tend to be a woman who works hard every day, in my own strength, self-directed and self-empowered. But as I learned to surrender control of my life and asked God to empower this new life, I began to live differently. I needn't be drained by self-effort anymore because of now living Spirit-dependent by faith. The power of God was flowing from my soul. This I wanted more than anything: to live under the control and power of the Holy Spirit. I simply asked Jesus to control and direct my life and surrendered, as best as I knew how, my right to my own life. I did what Paul outlines in Romans 12—making my body a living sacrifice—and began to realize I could live with God's strength and not my own.

On the drive home from North Carolina, I see an old restaurant that's absolutely crumbling. It's ugly, dilapidated, and hopeless, but some workers are around outside beginning some kind of renovation. On the building, a sign lights up the roof. It's the most wonderful sign I could have imagined. The words on this sign make me smile all afternoon.

The sign says simply this: "Come In! We're Under New Management!"

We're under the new management of a great God. The old has gone; the new has come and is coming.

We're surrendered, strong, and steady. "Under New Management" means whatever was left broken down, hurting, and hopeless gets a makeover. We're restored and renewed with God's renovating power.

Andrew Murray proclaimed: "[God] is able to let you rise from bed every morning of the week with that blessed thought directly or indirectly: I am in God's charge. My God is working out my life for me."[7] We are guarded by fresh, renovating, new morning kind of power. It surrounds us, infusing us and radiating from us. We can appropriate Christ's power by simply recognizing it's there, like the eagles flying on the thermals.

───⟨⟩───

I think about where I'll go and what I'll have to do today. I think about places and people that intimidate me. And then I remember my friend Rick's statement to me when I was worried about a presentation in the English department. He said, "Because you have Jesus dwelling inside you, when you walk into a room, you are the most powerful person in that room." I just moved from *fragile* to a *force* of mighty power.

This day just became really exciting as we remember what God's power accomplishes in and through us. God's power works in three ways that change how we experience our ordinary days:

We need His power within us to *produce* Christlikeness.

We need His power to *protect* us from sin and Satan.

We need His power to *proclaim* truth to others.

First we need power to be conformed to Christlikeness. We need the Holy Spirit's power in all the following ways. The Holy Spirit empowers us to:

become a new creation (2 Corinthians 5:17)
turn from worthless things (Psalm 119:37)
obey God's commands (Titus 2:11–14)
keep in step with God's spirit (Galatians 5:16)
thank God in all circumstances (1 Thessalonians 5:18)
love our enemies (Matthew 5:44)
forgive those who hurt us (Ephesians 4:32)

worship the Lord in suffering (Romans 8:17; Job 13:15;
   1 Thessalonians 1:6)

understand spiritual truth (John 16:13)

manifest the fruit of the spirit (Galatians 5:22–23)

encourage and *build up* others (1 Thessalonians 5:11)

give resources (Psalm 37:26)

offer hospitality (1 Peter 4:9)

esteem others (Philippians 2:3–4)

gain wisdom for decisions (James 1:5)

remember God's Word (John 14:26)

renew our mind (Romans 12:2)

live bravely (Deuteronomy 31:6)

intercede for others (Romans 15:30; Ephesians 6:18)

grow up in our faith (1 Peter 2:2)

know what to say (Luke 12:12)

have access to the Father in our souls (Ephesians 2:18)

follow God's purpose for us (Jeremiah 29:11; Acts 20:22)

reconcile us to others (Proverbs 16:7)

maintain a mind at peace (Romans 8:6)

use spiritual gifts to serve others (1 Corinthians 12:1–11)

and most importantly, *acknowledge* Jesus Christ as Lord
   (Philippians 2:10; 1 Corinthians 12:3)

We require the power of the Holy Spirit to *produce this Christ-likeness* in us, but we also need power *for protection*. It's God's *power* that activates each piece of the armor of God as Paul writes, "Be strong in the Lord and in his mighty power" (Ephesians 6:10) with the instructions for how to do so. We are to recognize six pieces of armor: the belt of truth, the breastplate of righteousness, the shoes of the gospel of peace, the shield of faith, the helmet of salvation, and the sword of the Spirit (Ephesians 6:13–17). We need this armor in order to "take [our] stand against the devil's schemes." It is not a flesh and blood struggle we are in, but a very real spiritual battle (Ephesians 6:11–12).

With God's power, we defeat accusations because we are guarded by righteousness. If you think of the image of the catapult and how we hurl ourselves confidently into God's presence, we can add detail to make the image even more vibrant: a breastplate covering you with righteousness. With God's power, we are guarded by peace. You can remember the smooth lake and how you move from harassed to harmonized, but now you recall the shoes that take that peace to others as you walk about your day. If you combine the shield of faith, the helmet of salvation, and the sword of the Spirit as decorations inside your soul's fortress, you have fortified your inner being with more than enough mental prompts to recall God's guarding strength in your life.

You also possess the eagle and the arm as reminders.

You are guarded by His power at all times, protecting you from enemy attack. When you feel assaulted in any way—from your circumstances, from your own mind, or from invisible spiritual forces of evil—call forth the truth that you are seated with Christ in the heavenly realms. In this seat, you wear the armor of God. Moving outward in your soul, your seat rests within a fortress that nobody can touch without God's permission. You are barricaded on all sides. You are guarded by power.

You are no longer fragile; you are a mighty force of Holy Spirit power.

Remember the arm. Remember the eagle. Remember the armor.

God's power guards you, and you turn from self-reliant to God-dependent. You lean on the great, strong arms working on your behalf. You soar like an eagle rising on the thermals. You fight like a warrior covered in heavenly armor.

Christ's power guards you, and you rest in the everlasting arms.

—⟋⟍—

We need God's power to *produce* Christlikeness, to *protect* us, and also *to proclaim*.

Jesus tells us to go preach the gospel to all creation (Mark 16:15), but His promise in Acts 1:8 that His followers would "receive power when the Holy Spirit comes on you; and you will be my witnesses" turned my world upside down. I felt my soul shifting toward an eternal purpose as I considered these statements. Wasn't my life purpose to earn the PhD, teach college literature courses, and live out my days with dusty books, poetry readings, and scholarly research about obscure nineteenth-century British poets?

Yes, but it was also so much more.

I decided I would see what the Bible had to say about purpose. As I was working on my PhD in literature, I simultaneously asked God about what it meant to have an eternal perspective and what His purposes for me could be. Paul writes,

Since, then, we know what it is to fear the Lord, we try to persuade others . . . that God was reconciling the world to himself in Christ, not counting people's sins against them. And he has committed to us the message of reconciliation. We are therefore Christ's ambassadors, as though God were making his appeal through us. (2 Corinthians 5:11, 19–20)

He had given us a purpose—a ministry—and it was called the ministry of reconciliation. God was "making his appeal through" you and me to other people to draw them to Himself.

God's power—that guarding power that clothes us from on high, that surrounds us and animates us with that strong, out-stretched arm, that lifts us high on wings like eagles riding on the thermals—isn't just for producing Christlikeness in us or protecting us from enemy attack. It is for proclaiming the message of Jesus Christ, reconciling all people to Himself.

You and I are a walking gospel proclamation. You and I are to be a billboard for Jesus Christ.

—⟋⟋⟋—

I can hardly find the words to explain how supernatural life became as I left for the University of Michigan and received the training I needed to proclaim Jesus in the power of the Holy Spirit *all day long*. I would talk to Jesus as I went about my day on campus:

Are You really reaching out to people through me, Jesus? Is this really happening? I will open my mouth and proclaim, but I'm not used to this. What's going to happen to me? Are You really with me? Is Your Holy Spirit really doing this because if not, I've lost my mind. I know I'm crucified with Christ and I no longer live but You live in me. The life I'm now living, I live by faith in You, Jesus, who loved me and gave Yourself for me.

Jesus says to His followers, "Follow me, and I will send you out to fish for people" (Matthew 4:19). If I recorded for you all that happened next as God sent me to "fish for people," I could fill another book. In short, God brought people to me, or He sent me to them, to tell them about Jesus. Everywhere I went, I talked about Jesus. During the first week when I was trusting Jesus that

He would, in fact, use me in the lives of people, I mentioned to my dental hygienist that I had been praying about how to afford a dental procedure that my insurance didn't cover, and she put down her cleaning tools and said, "You pray? You pray to *God*?"

"I do! And He listens and answers." Her eyes filled with tears as I spoke, so I asked her, right there in the dentist's chair, "Has anyone ever shared with you how to know God personally through Jesus Christ?"

"No. But I want to know!" she said as she hovered over my face in the dental chair. She moved my chair to the upright position as I dug into my purse and handed her a gospel presentation and scribbled my phone number on the paper. I told her about knowing God personally by receiving forgiveness of sins through Jesus Christ.

That night, the phone rang, and the dental hygienist said, "I read the booklet you gave me and prayed to receive Christ. Now what do I do?"

"Would you like to come to church with me on Sunday?"

She would. And she did.

In my office in the English department, students stopped in and asked, "How do I know the purpose of my life?" or "Why are you so happy and have so much energy?" or "I'm really struggling with depression, do you have any advice?" Each time, I'd share that my hope, purpose, well-being, joy, and enthusiasm came from Jesus Christ. I could then direct students to books and campus ministries to aid them on their spiritual journeys, and many of these students became Christians.

Those years as I earned my PhD transformed my thinking from a temporal to an eternal perspective. Everything about my work became about the eternal value of souls. God's power infused me with boldness and courage in the face of opposition, and His "divine power to demolish strongholds" (2 Corinthians 10:4) operated in my classroom and in my seminars.

Through God's power, I could proclaim biblical truth against the onslaught of postmodernism (no absolute truth), textual criticism (no reliable or authoritative texts), and anti-foundational teaching (the role of the professor is to call into question anything authoritative, traditional, conservative, or religious). In those years, God taught me that His power was always available, and I had nothing to fear. God was so kind to even allow me to have dinner with Christian apologist Ravi Zacharias, who spoke at the University of Michigan one evening.

During that dinner, Dr. Zacharias listened to my struggles as a graduate student and reminded me that the claim from professors who said, "There is no absolute truth!" was, in fact, an absolute truth statement itself. God used that special dinner to strengthen me in Christ more and more to stand up to the culture and proclaim Jesus in an academic setting. As I finished my PhD, instead of rejection and anger from the English department, I received heartfelt congratulations, teaching awards, and celebration from my colleagues who knew all about my faith in Jesus Christ.

If Jesus can do all that, He can do anything.

His power is unlimited and there is nothing He cannot do.

Now, nearly twenty years later, I move out in my day as a radiating presence of Christ. His power is at work to proclaim Jesus through me to others. His power defeats the enemy at every turn. I know this from my experiences of sharing Christ with Hindu and New Age neighbors who both responded to the gospel and prayed to receive Christ.

I've seen God's power to turn people from darkness to light in extraordinary ways. One neighbor, for example, had altars for worship set up in her home. She had been devoted to a yoga path that included the worship of various Hindu gods. On these altars, she had representations of these gods, New Age healing techniques, divination tools like angel cards, crystals, and bowls with money to act as an offering to find favor with Hindu gods.

When I began sharing Jesus with this friend, she added a baby Jesus figurine to her altar. After months and months—along with other Christians who cared about her—of reading the Bible with her, bringing her to church, praying with her, and talking to her about Jesus, I was so discouraged that she was still following her yoga paths. One memorable evening—sitting in the rocking chair—I was especially aware of the power of God, and I prayed that God, by His great power, would open this friend's eyes to the lies of the enemy and that He would expose deception and bring this dear friend to know Him. Could Jesus, by His power, give her a "spirit of revelation" to know Him?

The next evening during our neighborhood fitness group, this friend said, "I've been giving my money to all these practices for twelve years. It's not working. I have no peace inside. I have nowhere to take my sin. I think I have literal idols that I've been praying to, and I want to know Jesus."

ANYONE WHO DOUBTS THAT GOD SENDS CHRISTIANS ON RESCUE MISSIONS TO HURTING PEOPLE DOESN'T REALIZE THE POWER OF GOD TO ORCHESTRATE EVENTS BY HIS HOLY SPIRIT.

Another week, something so supernatural happened that I still can hardly believe it. I felt the Holy Spirit leading me to leave early for a lunch appointment and drive around the neighborhood. This was a strange moment for me; I'm an academic who believes she's theologically sound, rarely mystical, and suspicious of promptings that I can't confirm with Scripture. But I felt some kind of inward prompting to leave the house *now*. But it gets stranger. I felt led by God to wear a brown scarf that I never wear. It gets stranger. I felt led by God to put on Bruce Springsteen in the van as I left my driveway to drive around the neighborhood. I turned up the volume to "Hungry Heart" and backed out of the driveway.

Maybe I'm losing my mind. Is this You, Jesus? I'll do whatever You say, but this is really weird. No sooner had I turned left out of my driveway that I saw a neighbor standing on the corner crying. She was just standing there alone, crying.

I pull up beside her and roll down my van window.

She approaches me, obviously in distress, and says, "Oh, you're wearing the scarf I got you for your birthday! Oh, you're listening to one of my favorite songs! Can I get in?"

She slides into the van, and I'm so astonished when she asks what I'm doing in the van at that time in the neighborhood—wearing the scarf, listening to the song—that I say, "Jesus sent me to go get you."

We cried together and prayed in the van that day.

And I thought, *Anyone who doubts that God sends Christians on rescue missions to hurting people doesn't realize the power of God to orchestrate events by His Holy Spirit.*

The power of God was at work in this friend's life, so much so that supernatural things continued to happen. For example, she visited a psychic who told her that a "profound internal change must happen to her" for her to have a good life. But the psychic couldn't tell her what the profound internal change was.

I'm standing with her in the driveway, and I cry, "I know! I know! I know what the profound internal change is! It's Jesus who makes you alive in Christ and rescues you from sin!" Later, after another appointment with both a psychic and a Reiki healer, my friend said this:

"Both the psychic and the Reiki healer said they think my profound change has something to do with a door. But they don't know what the door is."

We're in the coffee shop and I cry out again, "I know! I know! I know what the door is!" I pull out John 10:9 (NIV 1984) where Jesus says quite perfectly—almost in a way I couldn't believe at that moment—"I am the door. Whoever enters by me will be saved." I also read Revelation 3:20 where Jesus says, "Here I am! I stand at the door and knock. If anyone hears my voice and opens the door, I will come in and eat with that person, and they with me."

"Well then," she says, "it's Jesus."

Later, when I told this friend about the book I was writing on how Christ guards our souls, she said, "I know exactly what you mean. Every morning I put myself inside a bubble of His care. I feel love, peace, hope, and power here."

I laughed and said, "You picture a bubble, and I picture a fortress."

When I begin the day thinking about God's guarding power in me, an ordinary person—producing Christlikeness, protecting, even proclaiming Himself through me—I find myself filled with awe, overwhelmed with the adventure this day will bring. The boring, unimportant, depressed kind of living I once dreaded dissolves each day into the reality of God's guarding power. I think again of the arm and the eagle. Then I remember: "His divine power has given us everything we need for a godly life through our knowledge of him who called us by his own glory and goodness" (2 Peter 1:3). We have everything we need. I lift my head from the pillow in the morning and stretch my arms up over my head. *This is going to be a great, powerful day.* I move from fragile to a mighty force of God in the world.

Someone once asked me why we so often fall back into self-effort and rely on our own power when God's unlimited power is available to us. I thought about that question and discovered the answer is the same as the problem of the Israelites.

We forget.

But how can I forget this power when I'm an eagle on the thermals, a soul animated by the arms and hands of God Himself, and a fragile person now turned into a mighty force? I'm fragile to forceful, flying on thermals, fortified in my fortress with the forelimbs of God. Oh, how I love alliteration. My writing students would be proud.

I return to Philippians 4:13: "I can do all this through him who gives me strength." His arms and hands enclose me; I'm guarded in that strong grip of God.

STIRRING OUR SOULS

—W—

1. Read Ephesians 1:17–20. How do we access the super-natural, unlimited power of God?

2. In what area of your life right now do you feel like you need to depend upon God's power and not your own strength?

3. Why do we fall back into self-effort each day? Give an example from your own life.

4. Think about the people in your life who do not know Jesus. Write down three names. Do you believe that Jesus sends you to "fish for people" and that you are "Christ's ambassador"? Read 2 Corinthians 5:11–21. How will your life change in light of this passage of Scripture?

CHAPTER 9

THE WIN SHOT: FROM SELF-OBSESSED TO SAVIOR-FOCUSED

You will be restored to your true humanity:
to be the human vehicle of the divine life.

—MAJOR IAN THOMAS

The more we let God take us over, the more truly ourselves we
become . . . It is when I turn to Christ, when I give up myself to His
personality, that I first begin to have a real personality of my own.

—C. S. LEWIS

Perhaps the most troubling words spoken by Jesus are these:

Whoever wants to be my disciple must deny themselves and take up their cross and follow me. For whoever wants to save their life will lose it, but whoever loses their life for me will find it. What good will it be for someone to gain the whole world, yet forfeit their soul? Or what can anyone give in exchange for their soul? (Matthew 16:24–26)

Following Jesus—to truly surrender everything—involves a *death to self*. You allow a complete divine takeover of your soul. You give up your right to direct your own life. You tell God that He can do anything He wants with you. You, like Paul, live a "crucified life" where you no longer live, but Christ lives in you.

Who would ever agree to such a transaction? Who would ever willingly surrender like this? Why would God ask for such a sacrifice, and what must be true about His character to make this request something loving and good? The benefits must outweigh the cost, or who would willingly abandon themselves to Jesus Christ?

As I think about the guarding presence of Jesus in my soul fortress, the next aspect of His character I needed so desperately to remember—beyond righteousness, peace, hope, and power—was the fact that I could escape from self-obsession to a truly Savior-focused life that stays "hidden with Christ" (Colossians 3:3). The temptation to exalt the self and live a self-centered, self-important life plagues us all.

Some years ago, at the height of my desire to make a name for myself, live a glamorous life, and continue in a narcissistic pattern of living, I read a quote from Pastor Neil Anderson. He wrote,

> Satan's primary aim is to promote self-interest as the chief end of man. Satan is called the prince of this world because self-interest rules the secular world.... Until we deny ourselves that which was never meant to be ours—the role of being God in our lives—we will never be at peace with ourselves or God, and we will never be free.[1]

Living a crucified life transforms us into what we were always designed to be: at peace with God and ourselves and truly *free*.

We become ourselves at last. We are more ourselves than we were before knowing Jesus. Charles Spurgeon explained this profound mystery as something quite expected and normative for the Christian experience. He wrote, "There are hundreds here on whom that strange transformation has passed, so that they are no longer what they were." He continued, "You cannot work this of yourself. No priest can effect it, but the Holy Spirit can produce it. He can complete it now, so great is His power—so divine."[2]

Reading Anderson and Spurgeon together provided great hope as I read the Scriptures about denying myself because I knew I *wanted* to do this, but I also knew I had no power in my own strength to die to myself. Jesus was giving me the power to surrender to Him, and I could now be guarded by the crucified life of Christ whenever self-centeredness returned.

Christ invites us to die to self and live a different life—one in which we become, as C. S. Lewis wrote in *Mere Christianity*, "truly [ourselves]" and that by giving ourselves up to His personality, we begin to "have a real personality of [our] own."[3] Think of the Blue Fairy bending low over Pinocchio with the magic words, "Little puppet made of pine, awake. The gift of life is thine"[4] or when the Skin Horse tells the Velveteen Rabbit, "Once you are real you can't become unreal again. It lasts for always." The Velveteen Rabbit, like me, wants to know "Does it hurt? Does it happen all at once?"[5]

It does hurt, and it doesn't happen all at once. But this is the best kind of hurt you'll ever know. Living a crucified life is a daily choice to let Jesus take over every part of you, including your desires and dreams. It includes telling Jesus each new morning that you belong completely to Him to use as He pleases. It involves yielding your right to yourself and giving authority to Jesus.

We die; He lives. As John the Baptist said, "He must become greater; I must become less" (John 3:30).

Dying to your pleasures, your right to direct your life, your pride, your self-sufficiency, and your deeply held dreams will mark the most beautiful, transformative moments of your life. You will meet Jesus at the point of each sacrificial surrender of yourself.

Consider the implications of a verse like Galatians 2:20; the Christian life is always an invitation to metaphorically die. Whatever life we would live as Christians, it should be a crucified life that is somehow no longer living in the old way but fully alive in Christ.

Almost twenty years ago, I wrote in the margin of my Bible, "I want the *me* that is *You*." In Christian therapy, I learned the concept of a "real self" and a "false self" through examining Galatians 5 and Romans 7. My counselor at the time told me something astonishing. He said that we often believe we are beyond hope, too complex and chaotic inside, and that our mental health is this mysterious, inaccessible, hopeless matter. He told me that with Jesus Christ, these matters of the mind become not only simple, but that the search for mental health was truly accessible and orderly.

I felt hopeful sitting there in his office. I felt ready for healing. Galatians 5:16–23 showcased the difference between a Spirit-filled life (the real, right me) and a life governed by the sinful nature (the false, disordered me). Paul says it like this:

So I say, walk by the Spirit, and you will not gratify the desires of the flesh. For the flesh desires what is contrary to the Spirit, and the Spirit what is contrary to the flesh. They are in conflict with each other, so that you are not to do whatever you want. But if you are led by the Spirit, you are not under the law. The acts of the flesh are obvious: sexual immorality, impurity and debauchery; idolatry and witchcraft; hatred, discord, jealousy, fits of rage, selfish ambition, dissensions, factions and envy; drunkenness, orgies, and the like. . . . But the fruit of the Spirit is love, joy peace, forbearance, kindness, goodness, faithfulness, gentleness and self control.

As I studied this passage, I noted how my flesh, the sinful nature, was first "in conflict" with a Spirit-filled life. This I felt. I felt that I was at war with *myself*. All the great literature I studied at the University of Virginia and the University of Michigan—Shakespeare, Dostoevsky, Tolstoy, Faulkner, Flannery O'Connor, John Milton, the British Romantics, Walt Whitman, the modern poets —all often illuminated *a heart in conflict with itself.*

In Paul's letter to the Romans, he describes himself in this way: "For in my inner being, I delight in God's law; but I see another law at work in me, waging war against the law of my mind and making me a prisoner of the law of sin at work within me" (Romans 7:22–23). Later, Paul explains that the "mind governed by the flesh is death, but the mind governed by the Spirit is life and peace" (Romans 8:6).

I asked Jesus to help me truly crucify the flesh and "keep in step with the Spirit" (Galatians 5:24, 25). I learned to confess to God those behaviors and attitudes stemming from my sinful nature, and I asked Jesus to once again empower and direct me by the Holy Spirit. Paul tells us that the "acts of the sinful nature are obvious," and for me they were predictable; when I was out of step with God's Spirit, I became obsessed with prestige, appearance, and money. I became angry, sullen, and self-absorbed. Instead of love, I had hatred. Instead of joy, I allowed the despair in. Instead of peace, I had anxiety. Instead of patience, I snapped at my children. Instead of kindness, I sought to have my own way. Instead of goodness, I failed to bless when I could. Instead of faithfulness, I was a wishy-washy, unreliable doubter. Instead of gentleness, I was abrasive and harsh. Finally, instead of self-control, I was an overeating, over-spending, over-talking mess. I made a list of all the ways I knew my "false self" presented herself, and I learned to confess and reorient myself to a Spirit-directed life.

But it was more than just keeping in step with God's Spirit. I was guarded by Christ's crucified life, and He was living His resurrected life through me more and more. I was tucked away, hidden in Him like a small creature burrowing into her mother's fur. I've exchanged this broken down, hopeless soul for a new life in Christ. He's living in my soul, and by faith, this is happening all day long. *I don't have to live this day on my own, because Jesus is living it through me.* I think of my soul as crucified with Christ. I think of how I'm now alive in a different kind of way. I think of the deadness—following Satan and the cravings, desires, and thoughts of my flesh. I think of now being *alive to Christ and not myself.*

DENYING OURSELVES AND FOLLOWING JESUS GENERATES THE LIFE FOR WHICH WE WERE DESIGNED.

As we think about this concept more carefully, we might remember that our old selves were crucified when we received Jesus' salvation; we have "passed from death to life," and "we always carry around in our body the death of Jesus, so that the life of Jesus may also be revealed in our body" (Romans 6:6; 1 John 3:14; 2 Corinthians 4:10). There's another kind of living, from our souls, that sets us free to truly live a Savior-focused life that keeps us worshiping, in step with the Holy Spirit, and desiring to make His name great and not our own.

Does this sound difficult or even sad, as if such living involves too much sacrifice and denial? I've learned this as perhaps you have learned: *denying ourselves and following Jesus generates the life for which we were designed.* You don't need to be scared or somehow concerned that you're giving up a better life to follow Jesus. You gain your real life when you deny it for Christ. John's gospel repeats the truth over and over again: "in Him was *life.*" Jesus Himself says, "you refuse to come to me to have *life.*" He explains that only in Him do we have life—without Him, "you have no *life,* in you," and He claims, "I have come that [you] may have *life,* and have it to the full" (John 1:4; 5:40; 6:53; 10:10).

We can't escape the concept that it is through Himself that Jesus is offering life, real life. He proclaims, "I am the way and the truth and the *life.* No one comes to the Father except through me" (John 14:6). Like Paul teaches young Timothy in 1 Timothy 6:19, may we "take hold of the *life* that is truly *life.*"

May we want the life that is truly life. God created us for this.

The concept of living this new, spiritual life is not complex and disorderly, highly therapeutic, or based on some inaccessible neuroscience. No. The Bible matter-of-factly proclaims: "God has given us eternal life, and this life is in his Son. Whoever has the Son has life; whoever does not have the Son of God does not have life" (1 John 5:11–12). Jesus' great prayer includes: "This is eternal life: that they know you, the only true God, and Jesus Christ, whom you have sent" (John 17:3). We have eternal life in us now, the life that is truly life.

What's even more marvelous is the concept that we are now "hidden" in Christ. We rest in the fortress of His care, hidden away. In Colossians 3:3, we read this: "For you died, and your life is now hidden with Christ in God." We're hidden with Christ in God.

We're sheltered here. We're covered by Him. Think of every enemy of darkness seeking your life. Do not fear! They can't find you because you are hidden in Christ.

I began to understand the cry of the psalmist who asked God to "hide [him] in the shadow of your wings" (Psalm 17:8). David knew that God would hide him as he says, "For in the day of trouble he will keep me safe in his dwelling; he will hide me in the shelter of his sacred tent and set me high upon a rock" (Psalm 27:5). In the midst of hopelessness when he claimed his spirit failed within him, David said, "I hide myself in you" (Psalm 143:7, 9).

For someone who didn't want to live a hidden life—but rather a famous, self-exalting, self-indulgent, glamorous, on display kind of life—agreeing that I was now hidden in God's fortress and that I could now make Jesus' name great and not my own challenged me at first. If I followed Jesus and led this crucified self, hidden in Christ life, what would happen to *me*? Thinking about living in this secret place in my soul where Jesus' guarding presence was changing everything, I came across Isaiah 45:3: "I will give you hidden treasures, riches stored in secret places, so that you may know that I am the Lord, the God of Israel, who summons you by name."

Hidden treasures. Riches in secret places. He summons us by name into this secret, hidden life in our inner beings. Here, He presents the riches of new intimacy with Him. He offers the hidden treasures and secret riches of His righteousness, peace, hope, power, and now, the treasures of a crucified life. As we have seen, we are guarded by the crucified life.

In our soul fortress, we're crucified and guarded from sin, self, and Satan. We don't need to think about life the same way; it's about Jesus, not us. It's about God's kingdom and not our own.

—⟨⟨⟨—

I recently met a photographer at a fundraising event. When I asked about his work, he casually mentioned that he was one of the official photographers for the Academy Awards and the Miss Universe Pageant. I couldn't contain myself: I confess that I'm obsessed with celebrity culture.

I love the glitz and glamour of Hollywood. I love award shows: the red carpet fashion, the acceptance speeches, and the introductory film montage that pays homage to the art of filmmaking each year. I can even quote famous lines from acceptance speeches, like when Jack Nicholson, who won best actor in 1975 for his role in *One Flew Over the Cuckoo's Nest*, said so coolly, "I'd like to thank, last but not least, my agent, who about ten years ago advised me that I had no business being an actor." And Sandra Bullock's great line for her *The Blind Side* Best Actress win: "Did I earn this, or did I just wear you all down?"

I had to know everything from this skilled photographer who, I thought, perhaps wished he'd chosen a different seat at dinner, but he seemed as engaged as I was as he listed out his favorite celebrity encounters.

"So what do you do, just stand there and take their pictures?" I asked as I tried to think of better, more sophisticated questions.

"Well, I'm actually in charge of the win shot. The last six win shots that went international were from my camera. I have them on my phone. I can show you the win shots."

"The win shot?" I asked, thinking he was saying "wind shot," like when the wind comes and sends a celebrity's dress flying. I pictured the iconic moment when Marilyn Monroe's skirt flies up from the subway breeze in *The Seven Year Itch*. Did this photographer stand next to the red carpet and wait for wind to send skirts flying?

"Yes, you know, the *win*. When they *win*. I'm there to capture the moment *when they win*."

He's swiping through his camera images on his phone to show me famous win shots. I learn that the win shot is the most important in this genre of photography. It's the moment the crown goes on Miss Universe's head and the tear begins to fall down her cheek as she clutches her flowers. It's the moment the actor takes the Oscar statuette, the most recognizable trophy in the world. As the photographer talked about the technical difficulty of capturing that authentic win shot, a film reel of win shots went though my mind. I imagined all those prizes our culture most values whether the sports accolades of the Stanley Cup, the FIFA World Cup, Olympic Gold, or the Super Bowl. I thought of those winners of Nobel Prizes and Pulitzer Prizes. I could hear the applause and the click of the cameras. I could see the flashing lights of those cameras in my mind.

I felt the old ache rise up in me as I saw all those beautiful, glamorous win shots. Would I ever stand in those places with photographers taking my picture? Would I ever have the admiration of the world? Where was *my* win shot? And for someone now guarded by Christ, hidden there in the fortress of His care, would I now ever have my win shot at all?

That night, I kept thinking about my win shot. I thought about everything I had ever accomplished in my life. Was marriage my win shot? Having children? Earning a PhD? Writing books? *Jesus, what are my win shots? What will make You say, "Well done my good and faithful servant"? What will make You put a crown on my head when I see You face-to-face?*

Tears formed in my eyes as I thought of this meeting and considered the stream of win shots He might choose from my life. I thought of snapshots from my life that Jesus would honor. And these moments had nothing to do with fame or achievement. They weren't glamorous or important to the world.

In each snapshot, the camera clicked, not when I was doing anything the culture values. No, the camera clicked when I was *surrendering to Jesus.*

First, in my bedroom as a little girl asking Jesus to come into my heart. *Flash and click.*

Next, a memorable day at the University of Virginia when, in tears, I asked God to take over my whole life and make me the woman I was supposed to be and then crying with my sister at Mill Mountain coffee shop. *Flash and click.*

Then, driving down a country road when I sensed God asking me, "Will you live the life I ask you to?" I say, "Yes, Jesus!" *Flash and Click.*

Those were the win shots. The greatest, most honoring, and most significant moments of life were those moments when I surrendered to Jesus Christ, turning my life over to His loving, guarding care.

THIS MOMENT COULD BE A RENEWAL OF YOUR SOUL, WHEN YOU REALIZE, PERHAPS FOR THE FIRST TIME, WHAT IT MEANS TO BE STRENGTHENED IN YOUR INNER BEING AND LIVE FROM A SOUL GUARDED BY RIGHTEOUSNESS, PEACE, HOPE, POWER, AND THIS CRUCIFIED CHRIST.

But there's another win shot. And I'm not in this picture.

The win shot God reminded me of that matters more than any other picture in all of history and the future of humanity.

It's this: Jesus crucified on the cross.

That moment of public display—that win shot—looked like a humiliating defeat, but it was the moment around which all of human history orbits. We read in Colossians 2:15 about Jesus "having disarmed the powers and authorities, he made a public spectacle of them, triumphing over them by the cross." In Revelation 17:14 we discover that the "Lamb will triumph . . . because he is Lord of lords and King of kings—and with him will be his called, chosen and faithful followers." We read that at this name, Jesus, "every knee should bow, in heaven and on earth and under the earth, and every tongue acknowledge that Jesus Christ is Lord, to the glory of God the Father" (Philippians 2:10–11).

In my soul fortress, I place the picture of Christ crucified. I hang the win shot on the wall, and I know that I'm forever guarded by this crucified life and hidden in Him. Because of this crucified life, I move from self-absorbed to Savior-focused.

I move from self-promoting to self-abandoned. I gaze at the snapshot and remember my life is not my own. I've been bought at a price of this shed blood (1 Corinthians 6:20).

The most important, glamorous moment of your life could be right now. At this moment you can ask Jesus to rescue and keep you and draw you forever into His guarding care. Or this moment could be a renewal of your soul, when you realize, perhaps for the first time, what it means to be strengthened in your inner being and live from a soul guarded by righteousness, peace, hope, power, and this crucified Christ.

But just like counterfeits exist for every truth in our soul fortress, the crucified life has its own deceiving opposite. Remember the deceptions:

Instead of being guarded by righteousness, we work harder to earn God's favor.

Instead of staying guarded by peace, we find other counterfeit agents of inner peace.

Instead of placing ourselves within the guarding presence of the God of hope, we try to find meaning and joy in external prosperity.

Instead of accessing the guarding presence of power always available, we resort to self-effort.

Finally, instead of living from a crucified self that stays hidden in Christ, we could move in one of two deceptive directions: self-denial or self-exaltation that presents itself as a form of godliness.

The first counterfeit to a crucified life is a suffering life, meaning we believe we are more godly and more special to God if we are suffering. So we might seek out experiences that deprive us of pleasure or comfort because we believe this is more godly and more pleasing to God. I once believed that the godliest person was the one always struggling, always sacrificing, and always miserable. My roommate at the time was driving me around town one day. She turned to me at a stoplight and said, "You really think

> "YOU REALLY THINK GOD WANTS YOU TO SUFFER, DON'T YOU? YOU THINK IT'S UNGODLY TO BE HAPPY, DON'T YOU?"

God wants you to suffer, don't you? You think it's ungodly to be happy, don't you?"

I did. Years later, my sister told me people who deliberately chose impoverished living as some sort of sacrifice were often making an idol of it; they lived in superiority to others because of how much they deprived themselves. She turned to me, took one look at my thrift-store clothing and said, "Get in the car. I'm taking you shopping." She put me into a dressing room at a trendy store and kept bringing me some new outfits to try on. "Why do you think it's more godly to look frumpy?" She laughed. "I grew up with you! You used to love fashion!"

That day, my sister reminded me how God richly provides us with everything for our enjoyment. Because I've been so fearful of a prosperity gospel mindset—using Jesus as a means to gain wealth—I couldn't embrace all the good things Jesus wanted to provide for me—that included a new outfit now and then—and the triumphant victory He wanted me to have each day *to be myself and enjoy His good gifts*. Even when I received attention for speaking and writing, I felt guilty and nervous about the new experiences and joys that came with these roles. But Christian friends called to say, "Enjoy this, Heather! Enjoy all that God is doing and bringing in your life. Enjoy the ways He is blessing you!"

I've learned that a crucified life, hidden by Christ and guarded by Him lives in the reality of constant provision, power, and well-being. This surrender to His care doesn't mean, by definition, suffering, poverty, and internal misery. It's a surrender to allow God to control and direct the circumstances and provision of our lives.

Surrender doesn't necessarily equate to suffering. When we are guarded by Christ's crucified life, we enter into that reality—being crucified and now hidden—and everything becomes about Jesus.

Our lives, whether externally prosperous or not, whether devoid of suffering or not, become aligned with Jesus and His plans for us.

The second tempting counterfeit to living a crucified, hidden life is a self-exalted life that masquerades as a surrendered one. It's a subtle corrosion found in churches, books, and worship songs that uses Jesus *as a means to exalt the self.* Instead of glorying in Jesus, we glory in our own selves, our own well-being, and our own emotional experiences. Jesus becomes all about making our lives great and meaningful. So by the end of a sermon, a book, or a worship

BY THE END OF A SERMON, A BOOK, OR A WORSHIP SONG, WE LEAVE FEELING, NOT LIKE JESUS IS GREAT, BUT THAT *WE* ARE GREAT, IMPORTANT, AND THE CENTER OF EVERYTHING.

song, we leave feeling, not like Jesus is great, but that *we* are great, important, and the center of everything. We worship ourselves instead of living surrendered and full of adulation for the living God.

The often imperceptible shift might go unnoticed, but you might have fallen into the temptation if you feel like you're always wanting more, seeking out new emotional experiences, overly concerned with God's great purpose for your life, and praying mostly about your well-being and prosperity. When I become this way, I reorient myself by remembering all that Jesus has done and is doing in my soul for His purposes, not for my own agenda. I recall the truths of His righteousness, peace, power, hope, and crucified life living in me. I remember His purpose for me for increasing Christlikeness and kingdom proclamation and discipleship, and I pray more for the church and unbelievers than I do for my own personal ambitions.

Jesus isn't a means to an end; He *is* the end. And when I'm living a crucified and hidden life, I can ask myself a simple question as a test to know if I'm truly following Jesus instead of myself.

At a training seminar, Darryl Smith, the national director for Cru High School, explained to the students how you know you're following Jesus. Smith simply said, "You know you're following Jesus because He leads you to lost people." I couldn't deny the truth of this statement because of what I knew Jesus was doing in the world. He tells His followers they will now fish for people (Matthew 4:19); He gives them power to be His witnesses (Acts 1:8); He tells us He makes an appeal through us to others (2 Corinthians 5:20); and He commissions us for global ministry (Mark 16:15).

Do you remember my first question on that day I read Psalm 97:10 in that old apartment? I wondered what God is guarding, how He is guarding it, and for what purpose. I learned what (my soul) and how (by righteousness, peace, hope, power, and His crucified life) and now I understood why I am still on earth being guarded by Christ. It was to experience intimacy with Him first of all. And second, it was to join Him in kingdom work of evangelism and discipleship.

THIS MOVEMENT OUTSIDE OURSELVES KEEPS US CENTERED ON JESUS AND THE CHURCH AND PROVIDES A SAFEGUARD AGAINST THE ENDLESS SEARCHING FOR NEW TEACHING AND NEW EXPERIENCES.

A crucified life that ends with self-exaltation and self-involvement isn't following Jesus' plan to seek and save the lost and to then make disciples. And this statement from Smith takes me outside of my own story and attaches me to the larger redemptive story of Christ and His kingdom. If our Christian life is always about "me"—my well-being, my prosperity, my purpose, and my own internal life—we're missing the outward movement of Christ into the world to seek and save the lost and to help others grow into maturity. This movement outside ourselves keeps us centered on Jesus and the church and provides a safeguard against the endless searching for new teaching and new experiences.

Paul writes that we've been given spiritual gifts to "equip [God's] people for works of service, so that the body of Christ may be built up until we all reach unity in the faith and in the knowledge of the Son of God and become mature, attaining to the whole measure of the fullness of Christ" (Ephesians 4:12–13). When we do this, Paul says that we won't be "tossed back and forth by the waves, and blown here and there by every wind of teaching" (v. 14).

It's true: as we dwell in the fortress of God's care, guarded by righteousness, peace, hope, power, and the crucified life, we can then help others take residency in the fortress in their own soul. Instead of that storm-tossed soul I inhabited that day I first read Psalm 97:10, I began a new fixed and stable life, grounded into an unshakable kingdom of God. Jesus Christ and His kingdom— within me and without me as I connect with others—comprises this new identity in Christ.

I've spent years understanding how to picture this place of God's Spirit within me. But now, the final question for each of us isn't just *Where do I place the Spirit*, but rather, *Where has the Spirit placed me?* Consider the incredible and mysterious claim in Ephesians 2:19–22 about what all this work to understand identity in Christ was always about. Paul writes:

Consequently, you are no longer foreigners and strangers, but fellow citizens with God's people and also members of his household, built on the foundation of the apostles and prophets, with Christ Jesus himself as the chief cornerstone. In him the whole building is joined together and rises to become a holy temple in the Lord. And in him you too are being built together to become a dwelling in which God lives by his Spirit.

You are I are seated with Christ in the heavenly realms, guarded by Him and in the great fortress of His care because we are "being built together to become a dwelling in which God lives by his Spirit." My soul's fortress is now "joined together" with yours and "rises to become a holy temple in the Lord." This represents a beautiful picture of our togetherness, our interdependence, and our fusing together of a million gleaming fortresses to make a dwelling together for God. First Peter 2:4–5 reminds us that we are "living stones" being built into a "spiritual house." We're told this:

> As you come to him, the living Stone—rejected by humans but chosen by God and precious to him— you also, like living stones, are being built into a spiritual house to be a holy priesthood, offering spiritual sacrifices acceptable to God through Jesus Christ.

Seeing ourselves as living stones because we are indwelt with our living Stone in order to come together as a holy nation and "special possession" of God turns us from self-obsessed to self-abandoned people who declare the praises of the one who rescued us and keeps us for His glory.

As opposed to spiritual practices that exalt and isolate the self,

Christianity delivers us from the captivity of self and positions us into a radical new community. We are *together* to glorify Jesus. First Corinthians 3:17 tells us clearly that "God's temple is sacred, and [we] together are that temple." We are a body held together (Ephesians 4:16). Jesus, who prays for us in John 17:23, reminds us that He is in us in order that we "may be brought to complete unity." The goal is interdependence, and together becoming a dwelling place for God by His Spirit. We are all bricks in this holy dwelling place. The goal is a fortified inner being to become a fortified dwelling together.

—⟋⟍—

As I read my Bible one morning, I stumbled upon a verse in Isaiah 58:10–11 where God says, "If you spend yourselves in behalf of the hungry and satisfy the needs of the oppressed, then your light will rise in the darkness, and your night will become like the noonday. The Lord will guide you always; he will satisfy your needs in a sun-scorched land." This passage deeply convicted me. It deeply troubled me. I knew that the ancient paths of the Lord invited me to spend myself for others, and yet, I was drawn more and more to solipsism, narcissism, and introspection. I could sit around and think about my soul all day and never get outside myself. My soul fortress was still all about me.

Fortresses and palaces in the ancient world didn't exist simply to bless the main inhabitant. Palaces in ancient Israel were indeed centers of power and administration but they were also built with banquet halls, courtyards, apartments, and great foyers for large numbers of people to gather. They often included storage sites for food and resources to bless others in times of famine. Some, like Herod's Jerusalem palace, featured pools and baths and accommodations for hundreds of guests to enjoy themselves and sleep in beds. Ancient Historian Josephus describes this fortress and palace as "wondrous" and the palace was obviously so spectacular that he said it "exceeds my ability to describe it." Josephus does recount the "large bed chambers that would contain beds for a hundred guests" in each room.[6]

Ancient palaces invited others in to protect, bless, celebrate, nourish, and provide rest to them. Think about how Christ is dwelling in you—as a fortress, refuge, and strong tower—and think about how to invite others into your life in a way that protects, blesses, nourishes, and provides rest.

> DO WEARY PEOPLE FEEL SUSTAINED AND ENCOURAGED IN OUR PRESENCE? DO THEY REJOICE BECAUSE THEY SENSE JESUS IN US?

When I was a newlywed, an older woman talked to me about how to make my heart a "sanctuary" for my husband and children. When people were in my presence, did they feel more at peace, more blessed, and more refreshed? Or did I invite them into a turbulent inner being marked by instability, selfishness, and a draining of energy? Was I so toxic inside that I drained life from others? Or did I radiate the indwelling refuge of Christ to others and invite them into a sanctuary?

If we think of our inner life as a fortress of Christ's righteousness, peace, power, hope, and crucified life, this directly translates into how we welcome others in. Can you imagine if, when others spent time with you, they felt accepted, at peace, empowered, hopeful, and without self-consciousness?

Paul in Philippians 1:26 talks about how he wants people to get excited about Jesus because they have spent time with him. Jeremiah recounts how God wants to "refresh the weary and satisfy the faint" (31:25). Let's pray to have the kind of inner being that offers His refreshment, to be like the one described in Isaiah 50:4 when the prophet writes, "The Sovereign Lord has given me a well-instructed tongue, to know the word that sustains the weary." Do weary people feel sustained and encouraged in our presence? Do they rejoice because they sense Jesus in us?

Because we dwell in the fortress of God in our inner being, we offer a weary world refreshment and a sense of joy because we represent the Living God to others. Just like the palaces in the ancient world that invited others in, our own lives should offer an invitation to others to rest and refresh in our presence. We know that "times of refreshing...come from the Lord" (Acts 3:19), and more and more, we allow Jesus to beckon to others through our lives to enter into this presence.

We are guarded by the crucified, hidden life in Christ, and from this fortress, we move out from ourselves to bless the world, to lead others to Jesus, and help others mature in their faith. We help build, brick by brick, the souls of other people so they, too, can live in the fortress of God's guarding care. Then they, too, can know the privileges in Christ that are ever present, always available, and never withheld. And when they forget this guarding God, we know how to lead them back to their own soul and remind them of all the ways Jesus Christ is with them. He's guarding, rescuing, and keeping them, and they can know this presence right now.

We remember the win shot of the crucified life. This snapshot transforms us from self-obsessed to Savior-focused, and we then move outward into society as agents of proclamation and blessing. Remember the win shot, and go to Galatians 2:20: "I have been crucified with Christ and I no longer live, but Christ lives in me.

The life I now live in the body, I live by faith in the Son of God, who loved me and gave himself for me."

We're guarded by the crucified life, and we hang the win shot of the cross on the wall of our soul fortress.

STIRRING OUR SOULS

—⟋⟍—

1. Read Galatians 2:20. What does it mean to be "crucified with Christ"?

2. When you imagine a life "hidden in Christ," do you feel comforted or saddened about your own life? How? Or do you have other reactions?

3. How would your daily life change if you saw your soul fortress as a place to welcome others in to bless, nourish, and protect them?

4. What are some symptoms of the "self-obsessed" instead of the "Savior-focused" life? Make two columns and fill in some qualities of each kind of life.

PART THREE

LIVING DAILY
IN THE FORTRESS

CHAPTER 10

—⟋⟋⟋—

LEAVING THE DUNGEON

He, that hath light within his own clear breast,
May sit' the center and enjoy bright day:
But he, that hides a dark soul and foul thoughts,
Benighted walks under the mid-day sun;
Himself is his own dungeon.

—John Milton, from *Comus*

Listen, listen to me, and eat what is good,
and you will delight in the richest of fare.
Give ear and come to me;
listen, that you may live.

—The Lord's invitation
to the thirsty in Isaiah 55:2–3

We've talked about the soul fortress. In contrast, let's examine a soul dungeon.

A soul dungeon is dominated by the prison guards of condemnation, shame, anxiety, despair, weakness, and self-absorption. Even as people who know Jesus and read His Word, we may forget how to experience Him as a guarding presence who rescues us from this dungeon and the accompanying mindsets and how He places us now under the guard of His righteousness, peace, hope, power, and the crucified life. We can be like the character in *The Pilgrim's Progress* who stays in the dungeon while the key to his liberty is right in his own heart.[1]

How do we leave? We leave the dungeon and enter the fortress by recalling the truth about our souls each new day. We no longer forfeit our experience of the privileges we have in Christ because we cannot remember or simply attend to the truth.

We know that God often works in our souls regardless of our awareness of it, but our ability to experience this working grace depends on our choosing to bring it to our conscious awareness. We practice attentiveness to truth all day long. This, too, however, remains a God-dependent process since the Holy Spirit will remind us of everything Jesus has said (John 14:26). Yet we also know in 2 Peter 3:1 that Peter writes "reminders to stimulate [us] to wholesome thinking." We have the Holy Spirit taking hold of God's authoritative Word, and we have reminders to aid this process. We depend on God's Holy Spirit to train our minds to position ourselves before truth each day.

We move through the mental cues—the catapult, the moat, the window, the arm, and the win shot of Jesus on the cross—to bring ourselves back to our greatest weapon of warfare and what deserves our attention: God's Word.

Five anchoring verses tether us to an entire network of truth. In your soul fortress, imagine all the Scripture that sets you free each new day:

On the catapult, write Romans 8:1: *Therefore, there is now no condemnation for those who are in Christ Jesus.*

On the moat, perhaps on a bridge nearby, write 2 Thessalonians 3:16: *Now may the Lord of peace himself give you peace at all times and in every way.*

On a window frame, write Romans 15:13: *May the God of hope fill you with all joy and peace as you trust in him, so that you may overflow with hope by the power of the Holy Spirit.*

On the arm, write Philippians 4:13: *I can do all this through him who gives me strength.*

On the snapshot, write Galatians 2:20: *I have been crucified with Christ and I no longer live, but Christ lives in me. The life I now live in the body, I live by faith in the Son of God, who loved me and gave himself for me.*

We have pictures and corresponding Scriptures, and alliterative words to cue even more truth.

Confident, not condemned.

Harmonized, not harassed.

Delighting, not despairing.

A mighty force, not fragile.

Savior-focused, not self-obsessed.

As we reiterate the memory techniques throughout the day, we find ourselves living from the fortress and not the dungeon.

—⁂—

This morning, I moved through the daily practice of building anew the refuge and the fortress of God so I could connect with Jesus and remember who I am through His Word. I sat on the foot of the bed, and felt the old, dark weight—the default state of sadness, of hopelessness, and of exhaustion all the way to my soul. But then I tear off these mindsets like dirty clothes and begin, layer by layer, to build up truth. I run down the list and ask Jesus what it is I really need. What part of Him do I need most in this moment?

Here is a beautiful explanation of why God names Himself "I AM" (Exodus 3:14). It's because the name invites our completion of this sentence. In other words, Jesus says, "I AM . . . exactly what you need." He is the great "I Am_____" that we meet afresh every morning. It's as if Jesus says, "What do you need from Me today? What is it of My guarding presence that you need most right now? I provide this and immeasurably more."

As I wrote this book, each week demanded a different sort of answer. Some mornings, I woke up feeling the weight of condemnation from some perceived sin—real or imagined. I ruminated about all the ways I was failing, how I hurt others, and when I sinned against God in action and attitude. Even though I had confessed my sin and repented—knowing full well that I was forgiven and cleansed, that He has removed my sin as far as the east is from the west, even that He remembers my sin no more—I still struggled. What did I need most in that moment?

Christ's righteousness. I'm guarded by it, covered in it, and secure it in. I move from condemned to confident because "there is now no condemnation for those who are in Christ Jesus" (Romans 8:1). One week I needed to access the catapult image in my soul fortress and remember the confidence I have to approach Jesus at any time, in any condition, no matter how much I've sinned. I filled in the blank: I AM your Righteousness.

But during another week I'd open my eyes to a new day and find the anxiety covering me like a suffocating fog. I thought about deadlines, the safety of my children, lesson plans, or any assortment of dangers, possible humiliations, oncoming imaginary illnesses, and muddled, overwhelming but abstract notions of doom. Anxiety makes no sense, and you can't think your way out of it because thinking is your problem.

So I remember what I need most: *Christ's peace that passes understanding.* I'm guarded by it, covered by it, and sinking luxuriously into it as I recall the smooth, calm lake in my soul fortress. The image of the lake provides the mental hook I need to usher in the Scriptures that I choose to believe. Jesus is my Prince of Peace (Isaiah 9:6); I'm guarded by peace (Philippians 4:7); the mind controlled by the Spirit is life and peace (Romans 8:6); and as a child of God, "great will be [my] peace" as promised in Isaiah 54:13. He is my peace! He is my peace! I raise my head from the pillow and inhabit the reality of what Scripture says, and whether or not my mind obeys or not, I *choose* to live from my inner being and not my over-firing mind. Slowly, I make my way to the shower, and I'm swimming in the calm lake. I'm taking thoughts captive; I'm receiving the Holy Spirit's peace for this brand-new day. *I AM your Peace.*

But the next week, I wake up to the ancient despair I know so well. It's that hopeless feeling that nothing will change. It feels like drudgery, like wading through sludge just to empty the dishwasher. Everything that once shimmered sits before me covered in dust and shadow. Depression's cruel cloak descends, and the accompanying demons of cynicism, regret, and hopelessness approach like the waves of the sea that could topple me and drag me into the riptide.

But the difference is Jesus is here, right here. I'm in the fortress of His love, and I'm guarded by hope. There's a window here to see the new mercies of Christ, the beauty of my surroundings, and the hope promised in Scripture for good things now and good things to come. I think of that window, and I fling it open. I remember my blog, *Live with Flair*, and how today the Holy Spirit will show me something wonderful if I just look carefully. *I AM your Hope.*

Yet another week, I'm bombarded by the overwhelming sense that *I cannot do this.* I'm not strong enough, clever enough, organized enough, or energetic enough to do what Jesus wants me to do. I admit it: I feel powerless and like a failure, and I live this life only by God's power. I remember I'm fragile, but because of Jesus, I'm now a mighty force. I think of His arm going before me like some animatronic prosthesis that's doing all the work, and I relax in my soul. The Holy Spirit promises power, and this is what I access, by faith, knowing I'm completely shielded by Him, inhabited by Him, and enabled from His power available to me. *I AM your Strength.*

My favorite way to remember my Guarding God these days is the win shot and the crucified life. I have nothing to worry about regarding my own life. The old, false me is dead; Christ is living within this new me. This characteristic of my Guarding God allows me to worship *Him* all day long and not myself.

We move into our day, inhabiting the soul fortress where He's dwelling inside us. All we've been longing for is here.

I tell my students what *begins well ends well.* We spend an inordinate amount of time setting up their essay introductions and creating beautiful thesis statements that the papers promise to argue. I want every single sentence in that introduction to shine and invite the reader into the promise of the paper. So much depends on how that writer begins.

It's another new day, and I remember my lesson to the students that things that *begin well end well.* I want to begin this day well, so I move through the images to remember the guarded fortress of Christ. But I realize my mind isn't helping. I don't know what I need. But I don't have to do anything but position myself in front of God's Word and let Him do the work.

So I do, and I pray this, often incorporating the very words of Scripture:

Jesus, Your Word says that I'll be blessed as I take refuge in You and that You are a shield around me. I place myself once again in the refuge and fortress of Your care for me. I don't know what I need. I don't know what to do, but my eyes are on You. I invite Your power and presence into my life right now to renew my mind and help me; since I don't know what I need, I invite Your mercy—in whatever form it takes for my good and Your glory—to fill my life and the life of everyone in this house today. Increase my faith to live out of the truth of my inner being, where You dwell by Your Holy Spirit. I want to cooperate with You today and use Your energy, which works powerfully within me. I choose to be crucified with Christ and let Your resurrected life live through me. Help me sow to please the Spirit today. Most of all, I want to dethrone myself in the fortress of my soul and let You take the throne today. I submit myself entirely to You for Your use today. I love You, Jesus. Amen.

We move into our day, inhabiting the soul fortress where He's dwelling inside us. Here, we become "mature, attaining to the whole measure of the fullness of Christ" (Ephesians 4:13) because we know *how* God is with us. We have everything we've ever needed. All we've been longing for is here.

The great biologist and Harvard professor E. O. Wilson claimed that, even as a young boy, he longed for something he couldn't name. As he examined the creatures of Paradise Beach—needlefish, blue crabs, sea trout, stingrays, and sharks—he wrote this: "I also hoped for more than sharks, what exactly I could not say: something to enchant the rest of my life."[2]

I have followed the enchanting call of philosophy and naturalism, of romance and indulgence and consumerism and distraction.

I followed what seemed like it might enchant the rest of my life—whether new relationships, experiences, locations, or ambitions. Every time, I ended up weeping quietly alone. Like Wilson, I knew something was out there to enchant me or else hidden deep within my soul, but what could that be? Nothing could enchant me and satisfy my deepest desires and longings until I met and surrendered to Jesus Christ. C. S. Lewis describes the feeling of finally being welcomed into this life by saying, "The door on which we have been knocking all our lives will open at last."[3]

We open the door we've been knocking on all our lives, and we find we're welcomed into a fortress where God Himself dwells. There we discover the catapult of His righteousness, a moat representing His peace, a bright window of hope, and the strong arm of His power.

But most importantly we gaze upon Him, the one who rescues and keeps us. We build up the fortress each new morning and worship this God who guards our souls.

STIRRING OUR SOULS

1. On this particular day, which facet of God's guarding presence do you need most: righteousness, peace, hope, power, or His crucified life?

2. What do people around you do as they look for something "to enchant the rest of [their lives]"?

3. How do you think your life will change in light of now knowing your Guarding God?

4. Write a prayer to Jesus as your Guarding God to worship Him, thank Him, and ask Him for what you need.

NOTES

Chapter 1: True Places

1. Dallas Willard, *Renovation of the Heart: Putting on the Character of Christ* (Colorado Springs: NavPress, 2002), 22.

2. If you read the psalms in the New International Version and note the references to these structures of protection, you'll find that *shield* occurs 19 times; *refuge* 43 times; *rock* 25 times, *tower* 1 time; and *fortress* 17 times.

3. David Brickner, a Jewish believer and executive director for Jews for Jesus, explains the symbolism of the Feast of Tabernacles in the article "Finding Jesus in the Feast of the Tabernacles," published on CBN.com. This writing provides helpful background and explanation of the festival's use of water and light to explain why Jesus' teaching created such anger and controversy during this festival. See www.1.cbn.com/biblestudy/finding-jesus-in-the-feast-of-tabernacles. David Brickner is also the author of *Christ in the Feast of Tabernacles* (Chicago: Moody, 2006).

4. Corrie ten Boom, *The Hiding Place* (Grand Rapids: Chosen Books, 35th Anniversary Edition, 1971, 1984), 211.

5. For images and more information about the Spafford family, see the Library of Congress's account of the tragedy at http://www.loc.gov/exhibits/amer icancolony/amcolony-family.html. Here you can also view Mrs. Spafford's own handwritten telegram in which she writes, "Saved alone. What shall I do." A daughter born after the tragedy, Bertha Spafford Vester, recorded that her father wrote "It Is Well with My Soul" on the journey Spafford took over the part of the sea where his daughters died. The Library of Congress writes, "Horatio Spafford wrote this hymn, still sung today, as he passed over their watery grave." In a letter to his sister, Rachel, Spafford wrote about this trip and the death of his daughters: "On Thursday last we passed over the spot where she went down, in mid ocean, the waters three miles deep. But I do not think of our dear ones there. They are safe, folded, the dear lambs." http://www.loc.gov/exhibits/americancolony/amcolony-family.html#obj8.

6. Victor Hugo, *Les Miserables* (New York: Signet, 2013), 225.

7. Hannah Whitall Smith, *The God of All Comfort* (New Kensington, PA: Whitaker House, 1980), 180.

8. Brother Lawrence, *The Practice of the Presence of God: The Best Rule of Holy Life* (Renaissance Classics: Createspace, 2012), 29.

Chapter 2: Rescued and Kept

1. Daniel Defoe, *Robinson Crusoe, 1719* (Pittston, PA: Penguin, 2003), 19.

2. John Steinbeck, *East of Eden* (Pittston, PA: Penguin, 1992), 131–32.

3. Andrew Murray, *Humility and Absolute Surrender* (ReadaClassic.com, 2010), 78.

4. Donald Miller, *Blue Like Jazz: Nonreligious Thoughts on Christian Spirituality* (Nashville: Thomas Nelson, 2009), 233.

5. Brad Bright, email message to the author, February 2, 2016.

6. See http://judaism.stackexchange.com/questions/53561/difference-natzar-and-shamar.

7. Murray, 130.

8. Charles Spurgeon, *The Sword and the Trowel: A Record of Combat with Sin and Labour for the Lord*, 1865 (London: Forgotten Books, 2015), 531.

Chapter 3: Refreshing the Memory

1. Dallas Willard, *The Divine Conspiracy: Rediscovering Our Hidden Life in God* (New York: Harper, 1998), 334.

2. Suman Deb Roy and Wenjun Zeng, *Social Multimedia Signals: A Signal Processing Approach to Social Network Phenomena* (Switzerland: Springer International, 2015), 161.

3. Dallas Willard, *Renovation of the Heart* (Colorado Springs: NavPress, 2012), 199.

4. *Aladdin,* directed by John Musker and Ron Clements, perf. Robin Williams (United States: Buena Vista Pictures Distribution, Inc., 1992).

5. Ivan G. Marcus, *Rituals of Childhood: Jewish Acculturation in Medieval Europe* (New Haven, CT: Yale University Press, 1996), 1.

6. Ibid., 7.

7. Betsy Sparrow, Jenny Liu, Daniel M. Wegner, "Google Effects on Memory: Cognitive Consequences of Having Information at Our Fingertips," *Science,* Volume 33 (August 5, 2011): 776.

8. Ibid., 778.

9. Mark Gatiss, "The Hounds of Baskerville," *Sherlock Holmes* (season 2, episode 2), UK, perf. Benedict Cumberbatch (Holmes) and Martin Freeman (Watson), BBC One, January 8, 2012.

10. Sir Arthur Conan Doyle, *A Study in Scarlet: The Sherlock Holmes Collection,* Book 5, 1887 (New York: Penguin 2001),11.

11. Ibid., 11

12. C. S. Lewis, *Mere Christianity* (New York: Harper, 2015), 203. Here Lewis writes, "You thought you were going to be made into a decent little cottage: but He is building a palace. He intends to come and live in it Himself."

13. St. Teresa of Avila, *The Interior Castle*, 1921 (Santa Cruz, CA: Evinity, 2009), 264.

Chapter 4: The Soul Fortress

1. Murray Bowen, "Differentiation of Self," Bowen Center for the Study of the Family, http://www.thebowencenter.org/theory/eight-concepts/differentiation-of-self/.

2. For a wonderful exploration of castles and fortresses that appear in popular films, visit http://www.castlesandmanorhouses.com/films.php?Order=Year.

3. Charles Spurgeon, *The Treasury of David, Psalm 90*, http://www.romans45.org/spurgeon/treasury/ps090.htm.

4. Hannah Whitall Smith, *The Christian Secret of a Happy Life*, 1870 (Ada, MI: Revell, 2012), 108.

5. Hannah Whitall Smith, *The God of All Comfort* (Chicago: Moody, 1953), 133.

Chapter 6: The Moat: From Harassed to Harmonized

1. Hannah Whitall Smith, *The God of All Comfort* (Chicago: Moody, 1963), 98.

2. *The Hiding Place*, directed by James F. Collier (Charlotte, NC: World Wide Pictures, 1975).

3. Smith, 12.

4. William Wordsworth, "Intimations of Immortality from Recollections of Early Childhood," *Complete Poetical Works*, 1888 (New York: Bartleby, 1999).

5. The Greek explanation of "peace" from Strong's Greek Lexicon, https://www.blueletterbible.org/lang/lexicon/lexicon.cfm?Strongs=G1515&t=NIV

6. Elizabeth Goudge, *The Scent of Water* (Peabody, MA: Hendrickson, 2011), 75.

7. Smith, 178.

8. Andrew Murray *Humility and Absolute Surrender* (ReadaClassic.com, 2010), 67.

Chapter 7: The Window: From Despair to Delight

1. R. C. Sproul, *Lifeviews: Make a Christian Impact on Culture and Society* (Grand Rapids: Revell, 1995), 121.

2. Strong's Lexicon, https://www.blueletterbible.org/lang/lexicon/lexicon.cfm?strongs=G4134&t=NIV.

3. Ibid.

4. John Piper, "What Is Hope?" DesiringGod.org, http://www.desiringgod. org/messages/what-is-hope.

5. The Centers for Disease Control and Prevention Suicide Data Sheet, 2015, http://www.cdc.gov/violenceprevention/pdf/suicide-datasheet-a.pdf reports data from *Substance Abuse and Mental Health Services Administration*; results from the 2013 National Survey on Drug Use and Health: Mental Health Findings, NSDUH Series H-49, HHS Publication No. (SMA) 14-4887, Rockville, MD: Substance Abuse and Mental Health Services, 2014. Available at http://www.samhsa.gov/data/ sites/default/ files/NSDUHmhfr2013/NSDUHmhfr2013.pdf.

6. See the official National Park Handbook, *Carl Sandburg Home* (Government Printing Office, June 1, 1983), 60.

7. Chuck Colson, in a speech recorded in the prologue to the album *Heaven in the Real World* and first track listing "Heaven in the Real World," Steven Curtis Chapman, produced by Phil Naish and Steven Curtis Chapman (Sparrow Records, 1994).

Chapter 8: The Arm: From Fragile to a Mighty Force

1. Dwight Moody, *Secret Power* (New Kensington, PA: Whitaker House, 1997), 12.

2. See *Practical Christian Living*, "a discipleship series designed to equip men and women to live a dynamic, supernatural life" (Orlando: Campus Crusade for Christ, 2013), in the chapter called "Power for Living," 43–49, where the authors explain that we are filled with the Holy Spirit by expressing our desire to be empowered by the Holy Spirit, by confessing any known sin, and by surrendering control of our lives to Jesus Christ. www.cru.org.

3. Andrew Murray, *Absolute Surrender* (Vancouver, BC: Eremitical Press, 2009), 52.

4. https://www.blueletterbible.org/lang/lexicon/lexicon. cfm?Strongs=G2673&t=NIV.

5. See "How Eagles Fly" on the Annenberg Learner website, an educator resource using Journey North, a global study of wildlife migration and seasonal change, https://www.learner.org/jnorth/tm/eagle/EagleFlight Lesson.html.

6. Major Ian Thomas, *The Saving Life of Christ* (Grand Rapids: Zondervan, 1961), 14–15.

7. Andrew Murray, *Humility and Absolute Surrender* (Peabody, MA: Hendrickson Publishers, 2005), 115.

Chapter 9: The Win Shot: From Self-Obsessed to Savior-Focused

1. Neil Anderson, *The Bondage Breaker* (Eugene, OR: Harvest House, 1993), 36–37.

2. Charles Spurgeon, "To the Rescue," (sermon, Metropolitan Tabernacle, Newington), published on Thursday, June 10, 1915, http:// www.ccel.org/ ccel/spurgeon/sermons61.xxiii.html.

3. C. S. Lewis, *Mere Christianity* (New York: HarperCollins, 2001), 227.

4. *Pinocchio*, dir. Ben Sharpsteen and Hamilton Luske. oerf. Evenly Venable. Walt Disney, 1940, film based on Carlo Callodi's *The Adventures of Pinocchio*, adapted into film by Aurelius Battaglia, William Cottrell, Otto Englander, Erdman Penner, Joseph Sabo, Ted Sears, and Webb Smith, RKO Pictures, February 23, 1940.

5. Margery Williams, *The Velveteen Rabbit: Or, How Toys Become Real* (London: Heinemann, 1922), 4. Full text with illustrations by William Nicholson at https://en.wikisource.org/wiki/The_Velveteen_Rabbit.

6. Titus Flavius Josephus, *The War of the Jews* (ca. AD 75), book V, chapter 4.

Chapter 10: Leaving the Dungeon

1. John Bunyan, *The Pilgrim's Progress*, 1675 (New York: Dover, 2003), 122–23. The text reads, "Now a little before it was day, good Christian, as one half amazed, brake out in passionate speech: 'What a fool, quoth he, am I, thus to lie in a stinking Dungeon when I may as well walk at liberty. I have a key in my bosom called Promise, that will . . . open any Lock.'"

2. Edward O. Wilson, *The Naturalist* (Washington, DC: Island Press, 1995), 9.

3. C. S. Lewis, *The Weight of Glory* (New York: HarperCollins, 1949, 1980), 42.

ACKNOWLEDGMENTS

Thank you to those who continue to pray for my writing and who journey alongside me as friends and Living Stones who together rise up as a holy dwelling place for God. I thank all those at Moody Publishers whose encouragement, wisdom, and diligent work turn my writing on overlooked verbs into beautiful books and audio recordings for others to enjoy. Special thanks for Judy Dunagan, my acquiring editor, whose passion to make God's Word come alive truly blesses the world; to Pam Pugh, the developmental editor who provided treasured insight and direction; to Rachel Heller, and the design team including Nathan Pernia and Erik Peterson for creating a stunning website and cover designs; to Kirsten Kamm, my publicist, for her wisdom, prayers, and direction; to Janis Backing who mentored me in the fine art of radio interviews and publicity along with Holly Kisly and Ashley Torres in marketing. Thank you to Adam Dalton for his encouragement and expertise. Thank you to the team at DC Jacobson who stuck with me. Special thanks to Mom and Dad for all their love and support. Thank you to Melissa Kish, who has always served as a guarding big sister and friend. Finally, thank you to Ashley, Sarah, and Kate who I place every day in the fortress of God's great guarding care.

ACKNOWLEDGMENTS

Discipleship Resources

978-0-8024-1382-6   978-0-8024-1459-5   978-0-8024-1340-6

Moody Publishers is committed to providing powerful, biblical, and life-changing discipleship resources for women. Our prayer is that these resources will cause a ripple effect of making disciples who make disciples who make disciples.

Also available as ebooks

MOODY
Publishers®

From the Word to Life®

*From the Word **to Life***

Moody Radio produces and delivers compelling programs filled with biblical insights and creative expressions of faith that help you take the next step in your relationship with Christ.

You can hear Moody Radio on 36 stations and more than 1,500 radio outlets across the U.S. and Canada. Or listen on your smartphone with the Moody Radio app!

www.moodyradio.org